HÉLÈNE BAUCHART

ENGLISH, **COOKING,** etc.
MES RÉVISIONS GOURMANDES...

SOMMAIRE

Unit 1	Coleslaw	6-15
Unit 2	Clam chowder	16-25
Unit 3	Fish and chips	26-35
Unit 4	Glamorgan sausages	36-45
Unit 5	Baked beans	46-55
Unit 6	Shepherd's pie	56-67
Unit 7	Chicken tikka masala	68-79
Unit 8	Dublin coddle	80-91
Unit 9	Apple & plum chutney	92-101
Unit 10	Lamington cake	102-113
Unit 11	Peach cobbler	114-123
Unit 12	Cranachan	124-134
Solutions		135

Ce livret vous propose de réviser votre anglais par le biais de quelques recettes anglo-saxonnes. Cette approche peut paraître contre-intuitive tant on ne compte plus les préjugés portant sur les goûts et aptitudes culinaires de nos amis britanniques et américains. Pourtant, la gastronomie de ces pays repose sur un héritage d'une richesse insoupçonnée, bénéficiant en outre d'un terroir auquel les chefs Jamie Oliver, Nigella Lawson, Delia Smith ou Gordon Ramsay ont redonné ses lettres de noblesse ces dernières années pour la Grande-Bretagne. Pour des raisons pratiques, nous n'avons retenu dans cet ouvrage que de grands basiques à la fois simples et délicieux, que vous pourrez rapidement reproduire chez vous.

Chaque unité de cet ouvrage s'articule comme suit :
- un texte de présentation du plat, suivi du texte de la recette en elle-même ;
- une partie exercices portant sur ces deux textes, intitulée **"Questions around the text"** (exercices tout d'abord en lien direct avec les textes, pour en tester la compréhension et travailler les points de syntaxe et de grammaire qu'ils permettent d'aborder, puis élargissant l'horizon en étudiant des exemples en lien indirect) ;
- une partie intitulée **"Vocabulary interlude"**, proposant d'approfondir le vocabulaire lié au thème de l'unité, mais qui n'est plus liée aux textes (vocabulaire généraliste, le plus souvent utilisable dans bien d'autres contextes que celui de la cuisine) ;
- une partie ludique et décalée, intitulée **"Back to work – Laugh and learn"**, proposant des anecdotes historiques ou civilisationnelles ainsi que des citations amusantes sur le thème de l'unité. Cette partie donne l'occasion d'un méli-mélo d'exercices sur des questions diverses, pour continuer d'apprendre et de réviser dans la bonne humeur ;
- une quatrième partie, intitulée **"End-of-chapter test"**, composée de quelques phrases françaises à traduire en anglais en guise de bilan, et pour lesquelles vous devrez mobiliser les mots-clés et les notions grammaticales abordés dans l'unité.

Il est recommandé de travailler ces unités dans leur **ordre d'apparition** car certains points (de prononciation notamment) peuvent faire l'objet de rebrassage au fil des pages.

Dans les **exercices de prononciation,** les sons apparaissent entre crochets. Ils n'ont pas été représentés par le biais de l'alphabet phonétique international, qui demande un apprentissage préalable, mais à l'aide d'une transcription littérale reposant sur des sonorités françaises les plus proches possible des sons anglais. Pour comprendre les prononciations mentionnées dans ce volume, il vous faut juste ces quelques précisions :
- l'accent de mot est indiqué par une ' devant la syllabe accentuée (ex. : '*table*, l'accent porte sur ta).
- le son du *u* de *duck*, qui se prononce entre [a] et [eu], sera représenté par [eu], pour ne pas mélanger avec le son [a] lui-même ;
- [eu] (en exposant) représente un son [eu] très bref (son le plus courant en anglais) ;
- les sons de voyelles longues sont représentés en gras ([i] son court, [**i**] son long) ;
- le son *g* de *girl* (comme dans « garçon ») est représenté par [g], le son *j* comme de *juice* est représenté par [dj], le son *j* de *usual* (comme dans « jus » en français) est représenté par [j] ;
- la prononciation du *th* est représentée par [TH] quand il se prononce comme dans *think* et [DH] quand il se prononce comme dans *the*.

UNIT 1

Let's start our little food journey with coleslaw – pronounced [*kohl slô*]. The word comes from the Dutch *koolsla*, which means *cabbage*. This dish is an import from the Dutch immigrants who settled in New York during the 17th and 18th centuries. In this respect, it is a typical example of how the successive waves of immigration have influenced American food habits. In a nutshell, coleslaw is a cabbage salad. It consists of a mixture of shredded cabbage and carrots with a dressing. The recipe is a subject of much debate: should it contain onions or not? Is it better to use red or white cabbage? Should the dressing be mayonnaise, sour cream or buttermilk? Whatever options you choose, it is always yummy and quick to make. Coleslaw is widely consumed in the summer, when its crunchiness is welcome, but it suits many occasions: it can be eaten on its own as a salad but it is generally eaten as a side dish though, especially at barbecues or in pub meals. It's frequently used to fill sandwiches as well. In the USA, buttermilk or sour cream are more commonly used. In Great Britain, it generally comes with mayo and it also contains onions. Some adventurers add some pickles, various herbs such as parsley, or even raisins. The recipe that follows is an adventureless version, as close to the most basic one as possible.

COLESLAW

INGREDIENTS

4 SERVINGS:
- 1/2 big white cabbage
- 2 medium carrots
- 2 small onions
- 1 teaspoon of salt
- 1 teaspoon of sugar
- 1 pinch of pepper
- 1 teaspoon of apple cider vinegar
- 5 teaspoons of mayonnaise (homemade or not)
- 1 teaspoon of mustard

UTENSILS:
- a chef's knife
- a food processor with a shredding blade (or a vegetable grater)
- a large mixing bowl
- a small mixing bowl
- a whisk

1. Shred the cabbage as finely as you want it to be, using your knife or your food processor.

2. Peel the carrots and shred them using a food processor or a vegetable grater. Transfer the shredded carrots to the mixing bowl with the cabbage. Do the same with the onions if you choose to include some.

3. Toss the shredded cabbage and carrots together.

4. Whisk the ingredients for the dressing together in a small bowl. Cut the sauce with the vinegar, the salt, the mustard, and the sugar according to taste.

5. Pour the dressing over the shredded vegetables and toss to combine all the ingredients, until all the shreds are coated.

TIP
The thicker the shreds, the crunchier your coleslaw will be.

UNIT 1

QUESTIONS AROUND THE TEXT

1. Dans ce texte résumant ce qu'est le *coleslaw*, séparez les mots à l'endroit qui convient et rétablissez la ponctuation quand c'est nécessaire.

COLESLAWISASIDEDISHOFRAWVEGETABLES
WHOSEMAININGREDIENTISCABBAGEIT'SAPOPULAR
SUMMERSALADINTHEUNITEDSTATES
ANDINGREATBRITAINWHEREITISOFTENEATEN
ATBARBECUESALONGWITHVARIOUSGRILLED
MEATSITCANALSOBEUSEDTOGARNISHSANDWICHES
THERECIPEDATESBACKTOTHEDUTCHIMMIGRANT
COLONIESONTHEEASTCOAST.

2. Vrai ou faux?
Cochez la bonne case.

VRAI   FAUX

a. Coleslaw is a baked dish.
b. For 4 persons you need a whole cabbage.
c. The dressing can vary.
d. Coleslaw is usually the main course in a meal.
e. Vegetarians can eat coleslaw.
f. The English recipe comes with grapes.

3. 'In a nutshell' (l. 6, 7) does not mean:
- **a.** broadly speaking
- **b.** barely
- **c.** basically
- **d.** by and large

4. Which reformulation of 'our little food journey' (l.1) is not correct?
- **a.** our little food trip
- **b.** our little food tour
- **c.** our little food travel
- **d.** our little food expedition

5. The Dutch come from:
- **a.** Denmark
- **b.** the Netherlands
- **c.** Germany
- **d.** Sweden

6. What does 'on its own' (l. 14, 15) mean?
- **a.** unaccompanied
- **b.** alongside
- **c.** alone
- **d.** all by itself

UNIT 1

7. What does 'coated' (recette, 5.) mean?
- **a.** cut
- **b.** covered
- **c.** mushy

8. *Yummy* (l. 12) est un terme familier dont les adjectifs suivants sont des synonymes, sauf un. Lequel ?
- **a.** delicious
- **b.** bland
- **c.** palatable
- **d.** tasty
- **e.** appetising

9. Le mot *dressing* a deux sens différents. Lesquels ?
- **a.** un pansement
- **b.** un assaisonnement
- **c.** une armoire

10. Barrez les adjectifs qui ne conviennent pas pour qualifier le *coleslaw*.
- **a.** warming
- **b.** refreshing
- **c.** crunchy
- **d.** crumbly
- **e.** creamy
- **f.** bitter
- **g.** raw
- **h.** sharp
- **i.** sweet and sour
- **j.** rare
- **k.** sliced

11. If you want it to be crunchy, you'd better cut it:
- **a.** thickly
- **b.** finely
- **c.** in thin slices

12. Passez *Let's start our little food journey* (l. 1) à la forme négative, en utilisant la forme pleine de *let's*.

....

13. Quel est le contraire de *adventureless* (l. 21) ?
- **a.** adventurous
- **b.** adventureful
- **c.** adventurish

14. Formez les deux mots suivants à partir du mot *adventure* et de l'un des préfixes/suffixes suivants : *dis-*, *mis-*, *-ness*, *-dom*, *-ship*.
- **a.** mésaventure/malchance : ....
- **b.** hardiesse : ....

15. *Consumed* (l. 13) est le participe passé du verbe *to consume*. Remettez les lettres dans l'ordre pour trouver le nom dérivé de ce même verbe.

TUMONCISPON ....

16. Complétez les espaces par l'article *the* quand son emploi est nécessaire.
- **a.** Peel .... carrots that we need for our recipe.
- **b.** .... carrots contain vitamins.
- **c.** My hamster loves .... carrots.
- **d.** The garden is dry, I need to water .... carrots.

UNIT 1

17. Vous préparez un *coleslaw* avec une amie et vous lui expliquez les étapes. Entourez la forme correcte.
a. I'm peeling the carrots.
b. I peel the carrots.
c. I have peeled the carrots.

18. Peut-on remplacer *which* et *who* par *that* dans les phrases suivantes ?   OUI   NON
a. which means *cabbage* (l. 2, 3)
b. immigrants who settled in NY (l. 3, 4)

19. Complétez les phrases suivantes en utilisant l'expression du présent qui convient : *présent simple*, *présent ING* ou *present perfect simple*.

a. When you .... (prepare) coleslaw, you .... (prepare) a salad.
b. We .... (not eat) onions this week. We've got a stomach ache.
c. .... you .... (need) onions to make coleslaw?
d. She .... (not approve) of onions in coleslaw.
e. Mum, we .... (always have) coleslaw! I hate it!
f. People .... (consume) coleslaw since the 17th century.
g. It can take years to finally make the perfect coleslaw. Practice .... (make) perfect!
h. How often .... (you buy) coleslaw? Every other week?
i. I .... (like) coleslaw but not the kind they .... (eat) right now.
j. This menu .... (come) with free coffee.

20. Complétez les espaces par *that*, *what*, *which*, *who*, *whose* ou Ø. Il peut y avoir plusieurs possibilités.

a. All .... I need is a nice plate of your coleslaw.
b. .... I don't like about coleslaw is the dressing.
c. The man .... you invited likes my coleslaw.
d. Many children do not like coleslaw, ... is not surprising.
e. There are many people .... don't like onions in coleslaw.
f. The recipe .... I prefer is the one using raisins.
g. Mike is the neighbour .... barbecues are such a success.

21. Complétez ces reformulations : donnez le nom composé correspondant à la description ou *vice versa*.

a. Apple cider is cider that is made from ....
b. A raw .... salad is a salad composed of raw vegetables.
c. A .... is a device that processes food.
d. A .... is a blade that shreds ingredients.
e. A .... is a dish that you eat on the side.

22. Entourez l'adverbe de temps qui convient.

a. I usually cook *during/for/while* two hours on Saturday nights.
b. People eat a lot of coleslaw *during/for/while* the summer months.
c. Please, shred the cabbage *during/for/while* I'm making the dressing.

UNIT 1

23. Reformulez l'énoncé *whatever options you choose* (l. 11, 12).
a. It .... matter what options you choose.
b. .... matter what options you choose.

24. Relevez deux *as* qui signifient « en tant que » dans le texte.
....
....

25. Entourez la proposition correcte dans les phrases suivantes.
a. You love coleslaw, just *as/like* me.
b. Nobody loves coleslaw *as/like* I do.

26. Peut-on remplacer *such as* par *like* en ligne 20 ?
OUI ☐   NON ☐

27. Placez les mots de liaison suivants dans la phrase qui convient.
UNLIKE/DESPITE/WHETHER … OR/ALTHOUGH/IN SPITE/EITHER … OR
a. You can use .... buttermilk .... mayonnaise as a dressing.
b. .... onion is an optional ingredient, it is generally used.
c. .... the dressing, coleslaw is still a rather light dish.
d. .... of the onions, your coleslaw does not taste too strong.
e. .... Americans, British people do not use buttermilk.
f. .... you like it .... not, we'll eat coleslaw for lunch.

28. Vrai ou faux ?

	VRAI	FAUX
a. *Sour* rime avec *pour*.	☐	☐
b. *Parsley* rime avec *journey*.	☐	☐
c. *Raisin* se prononce comme *reason*.	☐	☐
d. *Cabbage* rime avec *mirage*.	☐	☐
e. *Recipe* rime avec *catastrophe*, *karate*, *machete*, *sesame*.	☐	☐
f. *Let us* se prononce comme *lettuce* (laitue).	☐	☐

29. Entre les lignes 5 et 8, en plus du mot *salad*, deux noms ressemblent au français mais présentent une différence orthographique. Débusquez-les !
.... et ....

30. Corrigez dans la liste suivante les mots anglais dont l'orthographe est incorrecte.

address ....
envelope ....
acheive ....
accross ....
rhythm ....
miror ....

syrup ....
abricot ....
fonction ....
langage ....
luggage ....
aggressive ....

development ....
pronounciation ....
to pronounce ....
abreviation ....

UNIT 1

31. Classez dans le tableau ci-contre les mots suivants selon la prononciation de leur s.
MUSTARD/VERSION/BASIC/CLOSE/USED/ USING/SUGAR/OCCASION/CONSUMED/ALSO

32. Chacun des mots suivants contient une lettre muette. Entourez-la.

a. sandwich
b. knife
c. half
d. vegetable
e. should
f. suit

[SS]	
[J]	
[Z]	
[CH]	

VOCABULARY INTERLUDE

33. Remettez les lettres de ces différents types de chou dans l'ordre.

a. LAKE ....
b. EFUROWALLIC ....
c. COLBRIOC ....
d. SELSBRUS STOPURS ....

34. Remettez les mots dans l'ordre pour reconstituer les traductions suivantes.

a. Ce test était bête comme chou, mais il a échoué. Les carottes sont cuites pour lui !
HE/GOOSE/FAILED/TEST/COOKED/WAS/SOUP/BUT/HIS/IS/THIS/DUCK

....

b. Mêle-toi de tes oignons ou les choses vont tourner au vinaigre.
UGLY/OR/MIND/THINGS/YOUR/TURN/OWN/GOING/TO/BUSINESS/ARE

....

c. Ian a la moutarde qui lui monte au nez car Sam lui a dit qu'il avait des oreilles en feuille de chou.
EARS/BECAUSE/IAN/HE/CAULIFLOWER/SAM/TEMPER/TOLD/HIS/HAD/LOSING/IS/HIM

....

35. Entourez le bon terme.

a. In slang, *cabbage/carrots/onions* means money.
b. The promise of a reward to motivate someone is a(n) *onion/carrot/cabbage* and stick approach.
c. A(n) *cabbagehead/onion-head/carrot-head* is a stupid person.
d. Your *cabbage/carrot/salad* days is a happy period in your life.
e. To know your *cabbage/onions/carrots* means that you know what you're talking about.

UNIT 1

36. Reformez des expressions idiomatiques en reliant chaque début de phrase à la suite qui lui correspond.

- **a.** If something cuts the
- **b.** Mr Morgan is unpleasant
- **c.** If Tom is as keen as
- **d.** Danny is full of piss and

- **1.** he is as sour as vinegar.
- **2.** vinegar, he's very energetic.
- **3.** mustard, it will be fit for the job!
- **4.** mustard, he's very enthusiastic.

BACK TO WORK – LAUGH AND LEARN

As you know, cabbage and onions can cause stomach issues. So, you should not eat too much coleslaw if you are prone to bloating, particularly if you have a date coming. But there was a time when cabbage salad would have been the perfect lover's dish. Indeed, until the 17th century many doctors thought that flatulent food like cabbage and onions increased men's virility. They believed the 'wind' they produced gave them good erections and boosted their fertility. The belief vanished in the 18th century when knowledge of men's anatomy improved.

37. Par quoi peut-on remplacer *can* (l. 1) ?

- **a.** ought to
- **b.** may
- **c.** needn't

38. Entourez les verbes au prétérit dans le texte ci-dessus qui sont irréguliers et donnez leur infinitif.

UNIT 1

39. Comment se prononce le *-ed* final dans les mots suivants ?

a. believed   [d]   [t]   [id]
b. boosted   [d]   [t]   [id]
c. vanished   [d]   [t]   [id]

40. Entourez la bonne prononciation des mots suivants.

a. issue   ['ichiou]   ['issiou]
b. increase   [in'kriss]   [in'kriz]
c. stomach   ['stam^{eu}k]   ['stam^{eu}]

41. Complétez la reformulation du texte ci-dessous en plaçant les mots fournis à l'endroit qui convient.

MANLINESS/ADVISED/MAY/DIGESTIVE PROBLEMS/RAISE/
BROADENED/TEND TO/EASY/DISAPPEARED/YOU'D BETTER

Cabbage and onions .... cause ...., so .... go .... on coleslaw if you .... be gassy. Up to the 17th century doctors .... men to eat this kind of food because it was supposed to enhance their .... and .... their fertility. The idea soon .... because the understanding of male anatomy ....

42. Répondez aux questions portant sur cette citation extraite de *The Golden Girls*.

Station manager: Excuse me. Can I get your attention, please? I'd like to clear the air.

Sophia: Don't look at me, I haven't had a raw vegetable in six months.

a. Donnez la forme pleine de *I'd like*.

....

Qu'indique cette forme ?

....

b. The joke is funny because 'to clear the air' means two different things:
  1. mettre au clair une situation
  2. se frayer un chemin
  3. aérer, purifier l'air

c. Par quoi pourrait-on remplacer *in* dans *in six months* ?
FOR/SINCE/NEXT

d. When was the last time Sophia had a raw vegetable?
6 months ....

e. Complétez la reformulation suivante.
I haven't had a raw vegetable .... January.

43. Par quoi peut-on remplacer *nothing but* dans cette citation de Mark Twain ?

Cauliflower is nothing but cabbage with a college education.

NOTHING EXCEPT/ONLY/NOTHING LIKE/
MERELY/JUST/A FAR CRY FROM/
SIMPLY/HARDLY/NO MORE THAN/SOLELY/
POLES APART

UNIT 1

44. Répondez aux questions portant sur cette citation de Sarah Millican.

> *My mother told me, 'you don't have to put anything in your mouth you don't want to'. Then she made me eat broccoli, which felt like double standards.*

a. Quelle différence de sens se produit si on remplace *don't have to* par *mustn't* ?

b. The quote contains
  1. A sexual innuendo about oral sex.
  2. A double meaning of the word broccoli.

c. 'Double standards' means:
  1. l'appétit vient en mangeant
  2. deux poids, deux mesures

45. Reformulez cette phrase extraite de *Mrs Dalloway* de Virginia Woolf en utilisant *like better* au lieu de *prefer*.

I prefer men to cauliflowers.

46. Trouvez les lettres manquantes des deux synonymes de *fucking* (attention, vulgaire !) employé par exemple par Eddie Izzard dans cette phrase :

D .... NED

> *You say erbs, and we say herbs... because there's a fucking 'h' in it!*

.... OODY

END-OF-CHAPTER TEST

47. Translate these sentences into English.

1. Tout ce dont tu as besoin pour faire un bon assaisonnement de coleslaw, c'est de la recette qui vient de ma mère. Épluche les carottes pendant que je te la lis.

2. Bien que le brocoli ne soit pas le légume préféré des enfants, ils aiment généralement le chou-fleur, ce qui est étonnant.

3. La salade de pommes de terre et le coleslaw sont des plats d'accompagnement traditionnels aux États-Unis, mais on peut aussi les manger seuls.

4. Je ne mange pas de crudités comme le chou croquant en ce moment car j'ai souvent mal au ventre. Tu ferais mieux de faire pareil.

UNIT 2

1 'Let's get away from it all, let's take a powder to Boston for
2 chowder', is Frank Sinatra's invitation to his sweetheart. Clam
3 chowder is the epitome of New England comfort food. The name
4 *chowder* is said to come from the French term *chaudière*, the
5 iron pot soups or stews common around the 18th century
6 and made popular by the Breton fishermen who settled in
7 Newfoundland. You will find in chowder the very thing to warm
8 your cockles. It is a chunky and thick type of seafood soup that
9 contains fish or shellfish, salt pork, onions, potatoes, celery,
10 milk, and cream. Chowder can be eaten as a starter or as a
11 main course. Originally, chowders were not made only with
12 clams, but with any seafood available. There are many different
13 chowder recipes across the United States. The most controversial
14 variation may be the tomato-based Manhattan-style chowder,
15 which makes purists cringe – in 1939, the state of Main made
16 the use of tomatoes in chowder illegal! For vegetarians or those
17 who feel that seafood is definitely an acquired taste, chowder
18 also comes in vegetable-based versions, the most common of
19 which is corn chowder. Chowder is usually served with small
20 crackers called *oyster crackers*, whose name is deceptive as
21 they do not contain any oysters. They are called that because
22 historically they have been served alongside oyster soups, stews,
23 and chowders, but also because they look like oyster shells.
24 Chances are you're going to have a hard time finding some in
25 France, but don't sweat it! Good old croutons will do the trick!

CLAM CHOWDER

INGREDIENTS

4 SERVINGS:
- 60 g of salt pork (bacon or ham), diced
- 1 tablespoon of butter
- 1 stalk of celery, chopped
- 1 onion, chopped
- 1 bay leaf
- 4 potatoes, diced
- 1 kg of fresh clams (or 500 g of canned ones)*
- 400 ml of milk
- 500 ml of water
- 250 ml of thick cream

* If you cannot find clams, they are replaceable by scallops or prawns.

1. If you're using fresh clams: clean them thoroughly in cold water in order to remove the sand. Place them in a cooking pot over a brisk heat for about 5 minutes and stir occasionally. Leave them to cool and then remove the meat from the shells. Coarsely chop them, and keep the clam juice aside. If you are using canned clams: coarsely chop them and keep the juice aside.

2. Gently brown the pork in a large frying pan.

3. Add the celery, the onion, and the bay leaf, and gently brown with butter until the onion is translucent.

4. Add the diced potatoes, the clam juice, and the water. Bring to a boil, cover, and leave the mixture to simmer for about 20 minutes (until the potatoes are tender). Then add the milk and the cream, and stir well. Finally, add the chopped clams and cook for a few minutes.

UNIT 2

QUESTIONS AROUND THE TEXT

1. There are a few mistakes in this summary about chowder.
Find them and correct them.

Chowder is a thick and smooth meat broth, whose name has French origins. Clam chowder is typical of Newfoundland in Canada. At the beginning chowder would be made with clams only but then many variations were invented. In Manhattan for instance, people started making a vegetarian version of chowder using corn. Chowders are accompanied by small oyster-filled crackers called oyster crackers. You will not be able to cook this dish if you cannot find fresh seafood.

2. Les mots en gras (utilisés dans le texte ou la recette) ont été placés dans la mauvaise phrase. Remettez-les dans celle qui convient.

a. An **sweetheart** → .... of something is the best possible example of something.

b. A **available** → .... is a big shrimp.

c. A **epitome** → .... is a boyfriend or girlfriend.

d. If you **warm** → .... something, you find it unacceptable.

e. If you **cringe at** → .... your friend's cockle, you're making them happy.

f. Something that is **prawn** → .... is within easy reach.

3. Find the missing letters in the following definitions (words used in the text or the recipe).

a. A sc __l__o__ is *une noix de Saint-Jacques*.

b. __ho__ __ ughly means *completely, fully*.

c. 'Get away from' and 'take a powder' mean to __ __ cape.

d. Ch __ __ __y soup is thick soup with pieces in it.

e. Something is an a__ __uired ta__ __ e if you don't like it at first but learn to like it over time.

f. 'Don't __ __ eat it' means *don't worry*.

4. Entourez le terme synonyme de *'starter'* (l. 10) parmi les propositions, puis ordonnez *dessert, starter, main course* selon leur ordre d'apparition au cours du repas.

a. pickle

b. dressing

c. appetiser

Ordre :

1. ....
2. ....
3. ....

UNIT 2

5. Entourez la ou les bonnes reformulations de ces mots utilisés dans le texte.

a. To have a hard time (l. 24):   to have trouble/to have no problems/to feel like
b. Chances are (l. 23):   it is bound to/it is unlikely/it is highly probable
c. To make illegal (l. 15-16):   to outlaw/to forbid/to advise
d. To remove (recette, 1.):   to eliminate/to allow/to get rid of
e. To do the trick (l. 25):   to fill the bill/to work/to fail
f. Deceptive (l. 20):   peculiar/misleading/disappointing

6. Placez ces termes exprimant une opposition/restriction dans la bonne phrase : **YET/CONTRARY TO/THOUGH/UNEXPECTEDLY.**

a. ...., they are called 'oyster crackers'.
b. .... what you may think, they do not contain any oysters.
c. The crackers do not contain any oysters, ... they are called 'oyster crackers'.
d. The crackers do not contain any oysters, they are called 'oyster crackers', ...

7. Match each of these cooking instructions used in the recipe to its French translation.

1. Over a brisk heat
2. Coarsely chop
3. Keep aside
4. Gently brown
5. Bring to a boil
6. Leave to simmer
7. To cook

a. Faire cuire, laisser cuire
b. Faire revenir doucement
c. Faire bouillir
d. À feu vif
e. Laisser mijoter
f. Hâcher grossièrement
g. Réserver

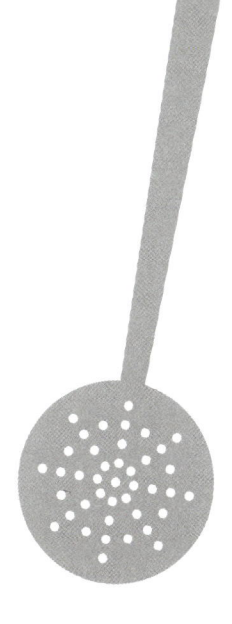

8. Déduisez la signification des trois faux amis suivants.

a. Yes, I'm sure. I **definitely** (l. 17) want to try oysters.
Definitely ne signifie pas *définitivement* mais ....

b. Chowder is not a stew, it's a soup **actually**.
Actually ne signifie pas *actuellement* mais ....

c. She may not like shellfish now, but she will **eventually**.
Eventually ne signifie pas *éventuellement* mais ....

19

UNIT 2

9. Trouvez le seul et même mot manquant dans toutes ces phrases.

a. The .... thing = exactly what is needed.

b. I bought the .... last bottle of milk; there wasn't a single other one left.

c. The accident happened before my .... eyes; I saw it myself.

d. That book was very long, but I read it to the .... end.

10. Sachant que *to look like* signifie « ressembler à » (à la vue), complétez ces traductions.

a. « Ils ressemblent à des huîtres » (au toucher) : they .... oysters.

b. « Ils ressemblent à des huîtres » (à l'odeur) : they .... oysters.

c. « Ils ressemblent à des huîtres » (à en entendre la description) : they .... oysters.

d. « Ils ressemblent à des huîtres » (au goût) : they .... oysters.

11. Fill in the blanks with one of these prepositions.
FOR/IN/OF/OUT/FOR/OF/FROM/OF

a. It smells .... chowder. I'm waiting .... Mum to serve lunch.

b. Oyster crackers remind people .... oysters.

c. *Meanwhile* means '............... the meantime'.

d. 'We're short .... clams' and 'we're running .... of clams'; both mean that we don't have enough clams.

e. Apart .... oysters, I like all seafood. Except .... corn, I like all vegetables.

12. Entourez la bonne structure.
Oyster crackers *have/are* a funny shape.

13. Précisez le sens de *any* dans ces deux phrases.

a. 'but with any seafood available' (l. 11-12)
....

b. 'they do not contain any oysters' (l. 20-21)
....

14. Put the sentence '*They are called that*' (l. 21) into the interrogative form.
....

15. Relevez deux expressions du futur dans le texte de présentation sur le *chowder*.

a. ....

b. ....

UNIT 2

16. Remettez les mots dans l'ordre pour obtenir une phrase au futur, puis attribuez-lui la bonne fonction :

1. action planifiée ; 2. décision spontanée ; 3. action imminente ;
4. déduction à partir d'indices ; 5. volonté ; 6. proposition.

a. to/cooking/start/am/the/I/about/clams: .... (…)
b. table/are/kitchen/on/clams/there/the/some   is/Mum/chowder/cook/to/going: .... (…)
c. chowder/we/some/make/shall? .... (…)
d. please/have/I'll/chowder/some/clam: .... (…)
e. dinner/making/our/am/party/for/I/chowder: .... (…)
f. the/help/cooking/you/with/will/me? .... (…)

17. Reformulez ces expressions du futur en utilisant *will* ou *be going to*.

a. It is not your plan to try corn chowder.

b. Do you feel like inviting the neighbours?

c. You do not intend to buy clams.

d. Do you want to make chowder?

18. Correct the mistakes in these sentences expressing forms of future.

a. When you will go to Boston, will you eat some chowder?

b. By the time you arrive, the children will have finish their soup.

c. This time tomorrow, we will had have chowder in Boston.

19. Cochez la bonne case.

a. *Bay leaf* et *bailiff* (*huissier*) se prononcent de la même façon.

b. *Replaceable* et *available* riment avec l'adjectif *able*.

c. *Prawn* rime avec *brown*.

d. *Vegetable* se prononce en quatre syllabes.

VRAI / FAUX

20. Placez ces mots selon la prononciation de leur graphie *ea*.

sweat – seafood – sweetheart

a. [i] ....
b. [â] ....
c. [è] ....

21. Devinez le mot mystère. Je figure dans la liste des ingrédients, mon **l** ne se prononce pas et mon second sens (verbal) signifie « suivre, traquer, épier quelqu'un ». Qui suis-je ?

UNIT 2

22. Circle the correct pronunciation.

a. iron   ['aï^{eu}n] – ['aïr^{eu}n] – ['aïron]
b. stew   ['st**ou**] – ['st**iou**]
c. epitome   [è'pitom] – [i'pit^{eu}mi]
d. acquired   [^{eu}'kouaï^{eu}d] – [^{eu}'kouid]
e. oyster   ['oïst^{eu}] – ['ost^{eu}]
f. said   ['sèd] – ['sèïd]
g. comfort   ['keumf^{eu}t] – ['komf^{eu}t] – ['keumfortt]
h. based   ['bèïzd] – ['bèïssd] – ['bèïsst]

VOCABULARY INTERLUDE

23. Trouvez la traduction anglaise de ces 13 noms dans la grille suivante.

a. coquillages et crustacés
b. homard
c. coque
d. moule
e. huître
f. calamar
g. oursin de mer
h. crabe
i. algue
j. crevette (deux possibilités)
k. écrevisse
l. poulpe

```
C O C K L E R Y A A U M
Z U P S E A W E E D Q A
Y S H E L L F I S H B P
C E U S Q U I D O X M R
X A S R E X E I H O U A
S U G C R A B S R C S W
H R M P Y C I E R T S N
R C H C Q F T E L O E K
I H R K Y S T G R P L B
M I V A B S M T S U R J
P N R O Y L G N O S L H
C C L O U V R R G J T B
```

24. Placez ces mots dans la phrase qui convient.

SOUP/CORN/OYSTER/CLAM

a. Tom is marrying Jane, he is as happy as a(n) ....

b. 'You earn your ....' means 'you earn a living'.

c. I have cleaned the whole house from .... to nuts.

d. 'The world is your ....' means 'le monde t'appartient'.

25. En changeant une seule lettre aux mots en majuscules, reconstituez l'équivalent correct de ces trois expressions.

a. As red as a MOBSTER
= rouge comme une écrevisse ....

b. To have thin SKIP
= être soupe au lait ....

c. Like a LIMPER to a rock
= comme une moule à son rocher ....

UNIT 2

26. Circle the right proposition.

a. If your cousin is a chowderhead, he is:
  1. lucky 2. stupid 3. smart

b. L'équivalent anglais de « se fermer comme une huître » est :
  1. to mussel down 2. to clam up 3. to shrimp away

c. If you're in trouble, you're in:
  1. the soup 2. the clams 3. chowder

d. La suite du refrain de la célèbre ballade irlandaise *Molly Malone* ('alive, alive, oh, crying…') est :
  1. lobster and mussels 2. oysters and cockles 3. cockles and mussels

BACK TO WORK – LAUGH AND LEARN

27. Détachez les mots au bon endroit pour former des phrases pertinentes, puis dites si les phrases a. et b. sont vraies ou fausses.

H E R E A R E T W O A S T O U N D I N G A M E R I C A N L A W S :
– I T ' S I L L E G A L T O S L U R P Y O U R S O U P I N N E W J E R S E Y, S O M I N D Y O U R M A N N E R S !
– I T ' S N O T A L L O W E D N O T T O D R I N K M I L K I N U T A H S O F O R G E T A B O U T Y O U R L A C T O S E I N T O L E R A N C E I F Y O U S U F F E R F R O M I T !

VRAI   FAUX

a. It's compulsory to drink milk in Utah.

b. It's illegal not to make noise while eating your soup in New Jersey.

28. Placez ces mots au bon endroit pour former un texte cohérent.

LIKE/A DAY/APHRODISIACS/RELIEVE *(MAKE FEEL BETTER)*/EGGS/CAREFUL/LATTER/STAMINA *(ENERGY)*

Oysters are famous as ....; they are supposed to give lovers sexual .... Casanova allegedly consumed at least fifty of them .... Be .... if you're offered prairie oysters or mountain oysters, though. They are not what they sound ....: the former are raw .... mixed with Worcestershire sauce, hot sauce, vinegar, and tomato juice; they are supposed to .... hangovers. The .... are sheep or calf testicles!

29. Expliquez le jeu de mots sur « *pulled a mussel* » dans cette citation de Billy Connolly.

So, have you heard about the oyster who went to a disco and pulled a mussel?

(indice : **mussel** et **muscle** se prononcent de la même façon, ['meuss^eul], et **to pull** a deux sens…)

....
....

UNIT 2

30. Entourez la connotation ajoutée par *do* dans la citation suivante, issue de *The Devil Wears Prada.*

> *Corn chowder. That's an interesting choice. You do know that cellulite is one of the main ingredients in corn chowder.*

a. une conséquence
b. une insistance
c. une addition

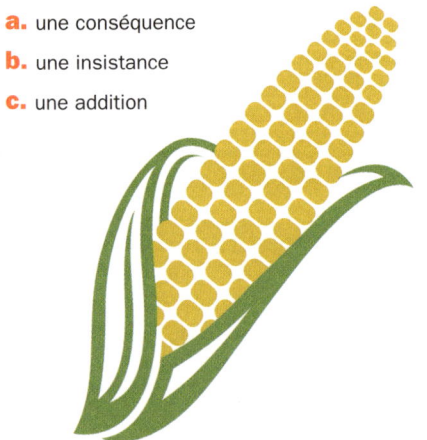

31. À partir des indices fournis, trouvez les synonymes de l'adjectif *main*, contenu dans la citation de l'exercice 30.

a. add one letter to CHEF ....
b. change the first letter to HEY ....
c. if you change my second and third letter, I turn into my opposite: M _ _ OR

32. Dans cette citation de Jonathan Swift, le mot en rouge présente une faute de frappe. Trouvez laquelle, sachant qu'il signifie *'brave'*.

> *He was a cold man that first ate an oyster.*

....

33. Entourez la bonne signification du mot *crap*, employé dans cette citation issue de *Kitchen nightmares* (Gordon Ramsay).

> *They've got it wrong on the menu. It's not a crab cake. It's a crap cake.*

a. dead **b.** funny **c.** shit

34. Remettez les lettres dans l'ordre pour trouver les synonymes de l'expression en rouge dans cette citation de Paul Neilan.

> *The world is your oyster... too bad you're allergic to shellfish.*

a. what a EMASH
....
b. what a TIPY
....

35. Entourez la bonne postposition dans ces reformulations de l'expression *up to you* utilisée par Chris Gardner dans cette citation.

> *The world is your oyster. It's up to you to find the pearls.*

a. It depends on/of/from you to find the pearls.
b. You are responsible of/from/for finding the pearls.

UNIT 2

36. Entourez la bonne proposition pour compléter ce proverbe chinois.

'Have patience, the grass will be milk ....'

a. enough early
b. enough soon
c. soon enough

37. Entourez la ou les expressions que l'on peut utiliser pour remplacer l'expression en rouge dans ce proverbe soudanais.

a. much worse with
b. better with
c. spoiled with
d. improved with

> The soup would be *none the worse for* more meat.

38. Placez les verbes *choking* et *digging* dans le bon proverbe.

a. There are more ways of killing a cat than .... it with cream. (proverbe allemand)
b. You cannot hook trout? Try .... clams. (proverbe chinois)

39. Reformulez cette citation d'Hannah Arendt en plaçant les mots suivants dans les bons espaces.

> No arguments can persuade me to like oysters if I do not like them.

CONVINCE/ABILITY/REASONING/EATING

'No .... has the .... to .... me into .... oysters if I do not like them.'

END-OF-CHAPTER TEST

40. Translate these sentences into English.

1. Si tu n'aimes pas les moules, je te ferai un *chowder* au maïs : l'exemple typique du *chowder* végétarien !

....
....

2. Ces crackers ont un nom qui prête à confusion et une drôle de forme, mais ils feront l'affaire !

....
....

3. Je suis sur le point de faire revenir des noix de Saint-Jacques. Laisse mijoter les palourdes pendant dix minutes et fais bouillir le lait.

....
....
....

4. Les crustacés ne plaisent pas d'emblée, mais tu finiras par les aimer.

....
....

5. Ne te referme pas comme une huître, tu es si jeune : le monde t'appartient !

....
....

UNIT 3

Fish and chips is a common takeaway food dish of English origin. It is composed of floured, battered, and deep-fried white fish – generally cod or haddock – accompanied by thickly-cut chips sprinkled with salt and vinegar. In England, it is generally served with mushy peas – peas boiled and mashed with salt and pepper – tartare sauce, a wedge of lemon to squeeze on top, and a good pint of ale or lager. An enduring symbol of Britishness, fish and chips is so deeply ingrained in English psyche that there's even a saying that goes 'as English as fish and chips.' The dish has been the national pride since the end of the 19th century, and it's still a classic on Friday nights. Over 250 million portions are sold every year in Britain. Most pubs have fish and chips on their menu, but people generally buy it from their local fish and chip shop, a.k.a. 'the chippy'. There are reportedly around 10,000 such shops in the country. For many years, fish and chips was wrapped up in old newspaper. The practice, which gave rise to the phrase 'yesterday's news is tomorrow's chip paper', was banned in the 1980s on health grounds.

FISH AND CHIPS

INGREDIENTS

4 SERVINGS:
- 4 haddock or cod fillets
- 200 g of flour
- 200 ml of beer (lager)
- 8 large potatoes
  frying oil (for frying the fish in a pan and for the chip fryer)
- salt, pepper

1. Make the batter: combine the flour and the beer into a bowl. Stir with a spoon until you get a thick and lump-free smooth batter. Leave to rest for about 15 minutes.

2. Preheat the frying oil to 120° C and prepare the chips: peel and cut the potatoes into thick slices.

3. Put the chips into the fryer for 10 minutes. Take them out of the fryer when tender but not yet golden. Leave them to cool.

4. Raise the temperature of the fryer to 180°/190° C and heat the frying pan.

5. Salt and pepper the fish fillets, then coat them with the flour and then the batter (in that order). Put them in the hot frying pan and fry until they get crispy and golden (about 10 minutes).

6. While the fish is being fried, put the chips back in the fryer at 180°/190° C for 2 to 3 minutes. Sprinkle with salt and vinegar.

UNIT 3

QUESTIONS AROUND THE TEXT

1. Correct the statements that are wrong.

a. Fish and chips is a dish you eat on the spot.

....

b. Salmon is not appropriate for making fish and chips.

....

c. A pub that has fish and chips on the menu is called a 'chippy.'

....

d. They stopped serving fish and chips in newspaper for environmental reasons.

....

e. Fish and chips is quintessentially English.

....

f. The dish used to be a Friday-night classic, but it isn't anymore.

....

g. The chips are fried twice at two different temperatures.

....

2. Complétez la grille ci-contre à l'aide des indices fournis (mots utilisés dans le texte et la recette).

Horizontal
1. augmenter (t°)
4. en purée (petits pois)
5. envelopper
6. reposer
7. quartier (d'agrume, par ex.)
10. asperger, arroser

Vertical
2. presser
3. pâte (à frire)
8. doré
9. croustillant
11. grumeau

UNIT 3

3. Écrivez en toutes lettres les nombres suivants.
- **a.** 19th ....
- **b.** 10,000 ....
- **c.** 250 ....
- **d.** the 1980s ....

4. Formez des noms composés à particule comme dans l'exemple fourni.

Ex. : take*away* food (l. 1) is food cooked and bought at the restaurant but taken home

AWAY/BACK/OUT/THROUGH/UP

- **a.** A break............... is an important discovery.
- **b.** A draw............... is a disadvantage.
- **c.** A check............... is a comprehensive medical exam.
- **d.** A run............... is someone who leaves without permission.
- **e.** A work............... is physical exercise.

5. Sur le modèle de *thickly-cut chips* (l. 3-4), construisez les traductions suivantes.

un cuisinier très qualifié ....
un sommeil bien attendu ....
de l'argent durement gagné ....
un ami au bon cœur ....
un voisin borné ....
des idées rétrogrades ....
du poisson mal cuit ....
un restaurant qui vient d'ouvrir ....

- **a.** poorly-
- **b.** a highly-
- **c.** a newly-
- **d.** much-
- **e.** hard-
- **f.** a kind-
- **g.** old-
- **h.** a narrow-

- **1.** opened
- **2.** earned
- **3.** fashioned
- **4.** cooked
- **5.** minded
- **6.** needed
- **7.** skilled
- **8.** hearted

- **A.** restaurant
- **B.** money
- **C.** ideas
- **D.** fish
- **E.** neighbour
- **F.** sleep
- **G.** cook
- **H.** friend

6. Assemble the right groups of letters so as to form the words used in the text.
- **a.** lasting: ....
- **b.** *cabillaud* in France, *morue* in Portugal: ....
- **c.** deeply-rooted: .... - ....
- **d.** mind: ....
- **e.** devoid of lumps: .... - ....
- **f.** more than: ....

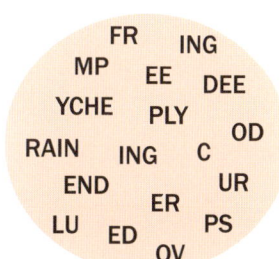

FR ING MP EE DEE YCHE PLY OD RAIN ING C UR END ER LU ED PS OV

UNIT 3

7. Entourez la bonne réponse.

a. *A.k.a* (l. 14) means:
1. area known as
2. as known at
3. also known as

b. A pale beer is a lager or a bitter, and a dark beer is:
1. a stout
2. a foster
3. a builder's

c. *On health grounds* (l. 18-19) means:
1. in hospitals
2. for health reasons
3. because of cuts in costs

d. What are *chips* called in the United States?
1. spuds
2. fries
3. crisps

e. *Yesterday's news is tomorrow's chip paper* (l. 17-18) is a phrase used to:
1. comfort
2. mock
3. threaten

8. Fill in the blanks with *in*, *at*, or *on*.

When I was a child .... the 1990s, there was a chippy .... my building and .... the end of my road as well. We would have fish and chips .... Fridays or .... weekends, generally .... the evening, ... 8 p.m. The dish was also .... the family menu .... lunch time .... my birthday – that is to say .... May 12 th.

9. Dans le texte de présentation du plat, relevez deux actions révolues et une qui continue dans le présent.

a. actions révolues : ....
....

b. action qui continue dans le présent : ....
....

10. Conjuguez les verbes entre parenthèses au *prétérit* ou au *present perfect simple*.

a. I .... *(run)* a chippy in London for ten years, from 1990 to 2000.

b. We .... *(just have)* some chips, we're not hungry.

c. People .... *(not eat)* potatoes until 1800.

d. I .... *(buy)* my fish on the sea front since 1998.

e. Tom .... *(take over)* a chippy a few years ago.

f. Mum .... *(forget)* her purse at the fishmonger's.

g. You .... *(be)* fitter since you .... *(begin)* eating more fish.

11. Entourez la proposition qui convient.

a. So far I .... tasted a better fish and chips.
1. still haven't
2. haven't yet
3. still didn't

b. It's the second time she .... cod from that fishmonger.
1. bought
2. would buy
3. has bought

c. .... you ever .... real English fish and chips?
1. have/try
2. have/tried
3. did/try

d. I .... you we needed more fish for tonight, didn't I?
1. did tell
2. have told
3. did told

UNIT 3

12. Fill in the blanks with *for*, *since* or *ago*.

a. I saw him a week ....

b. It has been a week .... I saw him.

c. I have not seen him .... a week.

13. Reformulez en utilisant un superlatif.

I have never eaten crispier chips.

Those are .... chips (....................)
....

14. Reconstituez trois phrases en plaçant ces six énoncés à l'endroit qui convient.

We can prepare fish and chips – They taste better now – I have bought fish – I have peeled the potatoes – I have salted the chips – You can slice them now

ACTION PASSÉE	RÉSULTAT DANS LE PRÉSENT
a.	.
b.	.
c.	.

15. Remettez les mots dans l'ordre pour former des phrases pertinentes, attribuez-leur la bonne fonction (habitude qui a cessé ou tendance au passé), puis reformulez l'habitude qui a cessé en utilisant *not anymore* et *no longer*.

a. I/child/vinegar/was/people/when/put/chips/would/their/on/a

....

b. wrapped/and/chips/up/used/be/fish/to/newspaper/in

....

Habitude qui a cessé : phrase n° ....   **Tendance au passé :** phrase n° ....

Reformulations :

c. ....

d. ....

16. Placez les mots suivants à l'endroit qui convient.

USED TO/SINCE/AGO/AM USED TO MAKING/FOR/HAS BEEN/ATE/DIDN'T USE/HAVEN'T EATEN/LAST/SINCE

a. I .... my own fish batter. I .... chips .... ages, ... I met you, in fact.

Yes, 2010 was the .... time I cooked some.

So it .... almost ten years .... I last .... some.

b. I .... to like fish, but now I do.

c. I .... smoke, but I quit eighteen years ....

UNIT 3

17. Apportez les adaptations nécessaires en complétant les espaces.

a. I **must** peel ten pounds of potatoes.
→ I .... ten pounds of potatoes **last night**.

b. Yes, we **may** use cod instead of haddock.
→ When we worked in a chippy **last year**, we .... to use cod instead of haddock.

18. Ask a question that is answered by the underlined information.

a. Fish and chips has existed <u>for two centuries</u>.

....

b. <u>Yes, I used</u> to like fish as a child.

....

c. I caught that fish <u>this morning</u>.

....

d. <u>No, I haven't</u> heard about that chippy owner <u>yet</u>.

....

e. The oil in the fryer needed changing <u>every week</u>.

....

f. I have lived <u>ten miles from the sea</u>.

....

19. Trouvez les mots mystères parmi la liste fournie, à l'aide des indices (un mot apparaît deux fois).

PALE/PRIDE/PEOPLE/PRACTICE/PHRASE/ SAUCE/ALE/WEDGE/SQUEEZE/WRAP/SALT/ TARTARE/PINT/PSYCHE/CENTURY/BATTER/ REST/PREHEAT/LUMP/SPRINKLE/FILLET / ACCOMPANIED/CRISPY/VINEGAR

a. Mon *p* est silencieux. ....

b. Mon *w* est silencieux. ....

c. Mon *e* final se prononce *i*. ....

d. Mon *t* est silencieux car je suis un mot d'origine française. ....

20. Find and circle the four statements that are right.

a. *flour* (recette, 1.) se prononce comme *floor*.

b. *accompanied* (l. 3) se prononce [^{eu}'keump^{eu}nid].

c. *lager* (l. 7) se prononce ['lèïg^{eu}].

d. le *ea* se prononce de la même façon dans *health* (l. 18), *death* et *breath*.

e. *raise* (recette, 4.) se prononce ['rèïz].

f. *banned* (l. 18) et *band* sont homophones.

g. Le *p* est muet dans *lump* (recette, 1.).

VOCABULARY INTERLUDE

21. Reliez chaque type de poisson à sa traduction anglaise (que vous devrez compléter).

a. morue   **1.** tr__ __t
b. truite   **2.** sea b__ __ __
c. maquereau **3.** wh__ __ ing
d. saumon   **4.** c__ __
e. raie   **5.** __ __ na
f. merlan   **6.** s__ __ mon
g. bar   **7.** macke__ __ __
h. thon   **8.** ska__ __

22. Find the words these riddles allude to among the list of words given below (some words are useless).

SMOKED/EEL/FISHTAIL/FISHMONGER/ FISHBONE/GILLS/SCALE/PICKLED/ RAW/FIN/TO SHELL/TO PEEL/TO SKIN

a. I form the fish's skeleton: ....

b. I am to fish what wings are to birds: ....

c. I am a way of preparing fish, often consumed as salmon in France: ....

d. I am the way in which sushi is eaten: ....

e. I am slippery, I look like a sea snake: ....

f. I am a verb that means 'décortiquer' when applied to shrimps: ....

UNIT 3

23. Entourez la bonne proposition.

a. An important person is a *big/small/queer* fish.

b. Someone who is strange is a *big/small/queer* fish.

c. A minor issue is just a *big/small/queer* fish.

d. Something suspicious is *fishous/fishened/fishy*.

24. Complétez ces traductions d'expressions proverbiales par *fish, beer, pea* ou *chip*.

a. Kate et sa mère **se ressemblent comme deux gouttes d'eau** :

Kate and her mother **are like two** ....s in a pod.

b. La lettre est arrivée en retard, **on est dans de beaux draps maintenant !**

The letter arrived too late, **we're in a fine kettle of** ....**now!**

c. J'ai eu cette voiture **pour une bouchée de pain** :   This car I bought **was as cheap as** ....

d. La vie n'est pas **un long fleuve tranquille** :   Life isn't all .... **and skittles**.

e. John **tient bien de son père** :   John **is a** .... **off the old block**.

f. J'ai **d'autres chats à fouetter** :   I have **bigger** .... **to fry**.

BACK TO WORK – LAUGH AND LEARN

25. Voici quelques exemples de noms amusants de bières britanniques, que vous reconstituerez en associant chaque terme à la suite qui lui convient (les traductions vous sont données en indice).

Indices : poule tachetée, doigts de l'évêque, coude du violoniste, couilles du chien, branleur rouquin, voleur de moutons, releveur de kilt, baiseur de moutons

a. Speckled
b. Ginger
c. Sheep
d. Bishop's
e. Kilt
f. Dog's
g. Sheep
h. Fiddler's

1. stealer
2. bollocks
3. shagger
4. hen
5. elbow
6. tosser
7. lifter
8. fingers

26. Les enseignes de *fish and chips* ont souvent des noms amusants. Essayez de deviner où se trouve le jeu de mots dans les noms de *chippies* suivants.

a. 'Our Plaice'   ....

b. 'Oh my Cod'   ....

c. 'New Cod on the Block'   ....

d. 'The Codfather' (indice : film)   ....

e. 'Chip 'n Tails'   ....

f. 'Frying Nemo' (indice : film)   ....

UNIT 3

27. Put the letters back in order in these two texts, then find the words the clues allude to in the grid.

A. *GINURD* .... the Second *DROWL* .... War, British soldiers would use this way to identify other soldiers as *ESEMINE* .... or allies: when a soldier would say 'fish' and the other answered 'chips,' he was an ally!

B. Eating *SHYMU* .... peas as a fish and chips *ESID* .... dish may not be the *SMOT* .... exciting thing *REVE* ...., but it will at least *RASPE* .... you the nightmare of the 'pea-eating *LURE* ....' advocated by good-manner guides: you *DUSHOL* .... never use your fork *SWADRUP* .... as a shovel but only downwards to spear the peas while using your *EFINK* .... for pushing. Just to be on the safe *DISE* ...., not of English etiquette but of American *WAL* .... this time, keep in *DINM* .... that it is illegal to fish from a camel's back in Idaho, to fish in your *SAPAJYM* .... in Chicago, and, *SALT* .... but not least, to have sex with live fish in Minnesota (no mention is made of *ADED* .... fish, though…).

Indices:

a. small word meaning 'en tant que' here ....
b. means 'épargner' ....
c. opposite of 'dream' ....
d. adverb meaning 'vers le haut' ....
e. means 'pelle' ....
f. means 'préconiser' ....
g. means 'secure' ....
h. set of government rules ....
i. someone who is on your side ....
j. principle of conduct ....
k. kitchen utensil used to cut things ....
l. desert animal that has one or two humps ....
m. no longer living ....

S	S	P	U	P	W	A	R	D	S	C	I
G	A	K	A	T	S	C	D	E	A	D	I
V	F	G	R	D	D	H	I	K	M	G	I
K	E	P	A	N	V	X	O	N	G	J	B
S	G	B	L	I	O	O	O	V	E	E	K
P	Q	M	L	G	A	G	C	N	E	J	N
A	B	U	A	H	F	C	L	A	R	L	I
R	I	R	T	T	C	Y	T	Z	T	L	F
E	A	U	J	M	L	N	A	S	G	E	E
L	Y	L	U	A	Z	A	C	A	L	L	Y
Z	P	E	P	R	K	Q	W	V	Y	Z	X
S	C	A	M	E	L	A	C	V	M	T	E

28. Apportez l'adaptation nécessaire à ce proverbe polonais si on l'écourte comme indiqué.

'Fish, to taste right, must swim **three times**
– in water, in butter, and in wine'
→ Fish, to taste right, must swim ....
– in butter, and in wine.

29. Donnez les adjectifs dérivés des noms en rouge dans ce proverbe allemand.

In wine there is wisdom, in beer there is strength, in water there is bacteria.

.... / ....

30. Correct the mistakes in the three rephrasings of the following quote from John Steinbeck.

There is nothing in the world like the first taste of beer.

a. The first taste of beer is the more delicious thing I have never experimented.

....

b. I still haven't experience anything better that the first taste of beer.

....

c. The first taste of beer is the lonely thing that feels as good.

....

31. Circle the funny word that is missing and which means 'not drinking any alcohol' in this quote from G.B. Shaw.

FLIBBERTIGIBBET / TEETOTALER / NINCOMPOOP

'I'm only a beer ...., not a champagne ....'

32. Entourez la fin de ce proverbe anglais très connu (signifiant que la beauté est quelque chose de subjectif) sur lequel joue Kinky Friedman dans cette citation : 'Beauty is in the eye of the beer holder'.

'Beauty is in the eye of the ....'

a. bee owner **b.** behaviour **c.** beholder

33. Entourez le ou les termes qui conviennent pour reformuler cette citation du boxeur anglais Ricky Hatton.

I've got a problem with my legs. They just can't walk past a chippy.

Hatton's legs can't *help stopping / be bothered to stop / stand stopping* when he sees a chippy.

34. Entourez la bonne proposition pour reconstituer ce proverbe néerlandais.

'When the beer *goes in - goes out*, the wits *go in – go out*'.

END-OF-CHAPTER TEST

35. Translate these sentences into English

1. Avant je détestais les petits pois en purée (mais plus maintenant).

....
....
....

2. As-tu déjà essayé de faire cuire tes frites deux fois ? Elles sont meilleures ainsi.

....
....
....

3. Je commandais à emporter quand je vivais à Boston, le vendredi soir surtout.

....
....
....

4. Le fish and chips est un plat qui a une part importante dans l'imaginaire anglais depuis son invention en 1860.

....
....
....

5. J'ai trouvé du saumon et du cabillaud pas chers au marché il y a quelques heures, mais je n'ai pas encore pu acheter de thon.

....
....
....

UNIT 4

Our next food adventure leads us to Wales. *Selsig Morgannwg* or Glamorgan sausages is a traditional vegetarian dish, whose main ingredients are leeks – no wonder, it's Wales after all! – cheese, eggs, and breadcrumbs. Because it allows you to use up stale bread and contains no meat, this very economical dish has been nicknamed the 'poor man's sausage.' Although they generally come in the shape of sausages, they can also be made as little cakes or fritters. In Wales, the sausages are sometimes eaten as part of a full breakfast including eggs, baked beans, and laverbread – kind of crackers made with oats and seaweed – or as a main dish alongside mashed potatoes or salad. Selsig Morgannwg is traditionally made with Caerphilly cheese, a sharp and crumbly variety of cheese named after the region it comes from in Wales. As it is not readily available outside Wales, even less so in France, the common advice is to use strong cheddar instead. Since much of the dish's flavour and texture relies on the cheese's crumbliness and sharpness, using a combination of feta cheese and parmesan is also a possibility that makes sense if you can't come by any cheddar either.

GLAMORGAN SAUSAGES

INGREDIENTS

4 SERVINGS, 2 SAUSAGES EACH:

- 70 g of butter (or about 10 tablespoons of frying oil)
- 2 average-size leeks, finely sliced
- salt, pepper, and nutmeg, to taste
- 225 g of breadcrumbs
- 2 teaspoons of thyme, chopped
- 3 eggs, separated
- 1 teaspoon of mustard
- 230 g of cheese, grated
- 3 tablespoons of milk
- 70 g of flour

1. Melt half the butter in a frying pan and cook the leeks until softened. Put in half the salt, pepper, and nutmeg.

2. Mix half the breadcrumbs with the thyme and the grated cheese, and stir in the leeks. In a separate bowl, beat the egg yolks and mustard together with the rest of the salt, pepper, and nutmeg, and add the milk. Stir well.

3. Shape the mixture into eight sausages and leave to rest for 15 minutes.

4. Meanwhile, whisk the egg whites. Put the remaining breadcrumbs, the flour, and the egg whites on three separate plates. Roll each sausage in the flour first, then in the egg whites, and finally in the breadcrumbs.

5. Fry in a pan for about 15 minutes, until the sausages are brown and crispy.

UNIT 4

QUESTIONS AROUND THE TEXT

1. Placez ces mots au bon endroit pour résumer le texte en quelques phrases.
LOOK/VEGETABLE/LIES/CHEESE/PREVENTS/LEEK/MEAT/WASTING

a. The .... is a staple .... in Wales.
b. The dish .... you from .... stale bread.
c. The recipe does not use mild or runny ....
d. Glamorgan sausages can also .... like little fritters.
e. Selsig Morgannwg is a dish that is .... free.
f. Most of the dish's success .... in the cheese's texture and taste.

2. Find and correct the mistakes appearing in the following table.

PAYS	ADJECTIF DE NATIONALITÉ	NOM DE NATIONALITÉ (SINGULIER, PLURIEL)
a. Wales	Welsian	a Welsh, two Welsh
b. Denmark	Danish	a Dane, two Danishmen
c. China	Chinese	a Chinese, two Chineses
d. Spain	Spanish	a Spanishman, two Spaniards
e. England	English	an Englishman, two Englishmen

3. À l'aide des indices fournis, trouvez dans ces devinettes cinq mots utilisés dans le texte de présentation et la recette.

a. Change one letter in **week** and I'm the symbol of Wales. ....
b. Change one letter in **shark** and I'm strong (cheese). ....
c. Change one letter in **folk** and I'm the yellow part in an egg. ....
d. Delete one letter in **boats** and I'm a type of cereal. ....
e. Add one letter to **tale** and I'm no longer fresh. ....

4. À l'aide des indices fournis, trouvez dans la grille cinq mots utilisés dans le texte de présentation et la recette.

a. used instead of a real name ....
b. algae ....
c. to make possible ....
d. easily breaking ....
e. 'muscade' in French ....

```
F A S E A W E E D
A N D N C H Y E T
N K I Z F M M L P
U W M C O F L Q D
T A Z I K E V D B
M I R D G N V L M
E S O S M X A S L
G F A L L O W M W
C R U M B L Y D E
```

UNIT 4

5. The words in bold characters (used in the text or the recipe) have been placed in the wrong sentence. Put each back in the sentence it belongs to.

a. makes sense → .... your leeks means using your leeks completely, finishing them.

b. Buying things in bulk is reasonable and convenient. It **come by** → ....

c. If leeks are not **piece of** (i.e. easily) → .... available, buy onions.

d. I could not **using up** → .... any cheddar at the market; I didn't find any cheese actually.

e. This piece of cheese is **readily** → .... size; so are the eggs, medium size.

f. Replacing the Welsh cheese with cheddar was a good **average** → .... advice.

6. Entourez la ou les bonnes propositions.

a. *So* dans *even less so* (l. 14-15) renvoie à :
   1. *sharp and crumbly*
   2. *readily available*

b. *Since* (l. 16) means:
   1. because
   2. as
   3. during

c. *No wonder* (l. 3) could be replaced with:
   1. disappointingly
   2. expectedly
   3. unsurprisingly

d. *Economical* (l. 5) is the opposite of:
   1. expensive
   2. aloof
   3. costly

e. *No wonder, it's Wales after all!* (l. 3) is used because:
   1. The leek is the symbol of Wales
   2. The leek was first cultivated in Wales

7. Circle the five adjectives whose endings are not correct.

dramatic, academical, artistic, domestic, strategic, energetical, fantastic, majestical, linguistic, pathetic, tragic, biologic, critical, cynical, grammatic, medical, radical, physical, topical, tactical, economical.

8. Conjugate the verbs in parenthesis using either the *preterit* (*simple* or *ing*) or the *present perfect* (*simple* or *ing*).

a. I .... *(cook)* when you .... *(call)*.

b. She .... *(have)* this car since 2002.

c. The guests .... *(eat up)* all the leeks; there are none left.

d. We .... *(fry)* sausages; it smells delicious!

e. I .... *(live)* here for two months.

f. I had already left when you .... *(arrive)*.

9. Remettez les blocs de mots dans l'ordre pour former des phrases pertinentes et proposez une traduction.

a. forgotten the cheese/the sausages/I had/ when I realized/were already sizzling

....

b. I had/it was/made Glamorgan sausages/ the first time

....

c. able to/Caerphilly cheese/cook real Glamorgan sausages/there was/so I was

....

d. without tearing/when I/chop leeks/I could/ was younger

....

e. you been/lately/what have/doing?

....

f. Welsh food/she has/this month/twice/prepared

....

UNIT 4

10. Parmi la liste suivante, trouvez le ou les mots concernés par les petites devinettes qui suivent.

SAUSAGE/STALE/MEAT/AVAILABLE/BREADCRUMB/INSTEAD/ALTHOUGH/EITHER/WEED/ FRITTER/YOLK/WALES/CRUMBLY/SLICED/MILK/FLOUR/MELT/HALF/MEANWHILE/THYME

a. Mon *b* est silencieux. ....
b. Notre *l* est silencieux. ....
c. Je rime avec *bridge* mais pas avec *page*. ....
d. Mon *th* se prononce comme celui de *Thai* et *Thames*. ....

11. Trouvez quels mots utilisés dans le texte de présentation ou la recette sont homophones des mots suggérés par les indices.

INDICE	HOMOPHONE DE MOTS DU TEXTE	MOT DU TEXTE CONCERNÉ
a. sixty minutes	hour	our (l. 1)
b. to see for the first time		
c. root used to make sugar		
d. means 'verser'		
e. means 'domestique'		
f. horse's hair		
g. measured in hours, days, years		
h. means 'fuite'		
i. can be a rose, a tulip, etc.		

12. Entourez l'intonation qu'il faut prendre (montante ou descendante) pour prononcer les phrases suivantes (attention la phrase e. demande une modulation).

a. Is Glamorgan sausages a Welsh recipe?   ↑ ↓
b. Why are you chopping leeks?   ↑ ↓
c. Glamorgan sausages is a traditional vegetarian dish.   ↑ ↓
d. Don't put cheddar in the sausage!   ↑ ↓
e. … leeks, cheese, eggs, breadcrumbs, and milk. (*énumération*)   ↑ ↓

VOCABULARY INTERLUDE

13. Trouvez les lettres manquantes dans la traduction de ces noms d'herbes aromatiques.

a. Romarin :   _O_EMA_Y
b. Origan :   OR_GAN_
c. Estragon :   TAR_ _GON

UNIT 4

14. Place the following words in the correct line, according to what they apply to.

Adjectifs : wholegrain, runny, leavened, crumbly, scrambled, sharp, mild, hard-boiled, pungent, hard, sliced, crusty, spreadable, creamy, sunny side up, blue, ripe, moldy, melted, aged, poached, soft boiled, over easy, fried, stale.

Noms : wheel, shell, toast, block, soldiers, lump, brick, bun, log, slice, yolk, loaf, crumb, wedge, slab, roll.

a. Cheese ....

b. Egg ....

c. Bread ....

15. Match each sentence with its ending.

a. Sam and I have nothing in common, we are •

b. Forget about it, it's no use crying over •

c. This phone app is so great! The best thing since •

d. In English 'on n'apprend pas à un singe à faire des grimaces' is *You can't teach grandma to suck* •

e. Oh my God, this romantic comedy is so •

• **1.** sliced bread!

• **2.** eggs.

• **3.** chalk and cheese.

• **4.** cheesy!

• **5.** spilt milk.

16. Placez les mots suivants dans la bonne phrase.

CHEESE/BREAD/SAUSAGE/EGG

a. You need spiritual things in your life, Sam! Man cannot live by .... alone!

b. Paddy was very embarrassed. He had .... on his face.

c. Emma did not pass her exam. Hard ....!

d. I have zero money left, not a(n) ....

17. Circle the correct proposition.

a. It stinks in here. Who has just farted? Who cut the *cheese/egg/leek*?!

b. Nessa is pregnant, she has a(n) *cheese/egg/bun* in the oven.

c. This job is important. It is my bread and *cheese/butter/sausage*.

d. Seeing him write his song made it less sexy. It was like watching *bread/cheese/sausage* getting made.

UNIT 4

BACK TO WORK – LAUGH AND LEARN

18. Correct the mistakes in the following text.

Sausages look as penises and where it comes to sausage-related sexuals euphemisms, we are all sudenly back

to be silly twelve-years-olds once again. In many languages the word *sausage* has sexual connotations.

English is not exception and 'to hid the sausage' for instence means 'to have sex' (nudge nudge, wink wink…).

Now that you know these essential informations, let's continue with funny cheese facts, shall we?

19. Circle the correct rephrasing of each term used in the text from exercise 18.

a. suddenly = of all a sudden/all of a sudden/a sudden of all

b. to have sex = to have (sexual) intercourse/to have (sexual) innermost

c. to continue = to move in/to move out/to move on

20. Vrai ou faux ? Cochez la bonne case.

	VRAI	FAUX
a. *Euphemism* se prononce [eu'phimizeum].		
b. *Penis* rime avec *famous*.		
c. *Penises* rime avec *sausages*.		
d. Le *u* de *nudge* se prononce comme le *o* de *comes*.		

21. Read the following text and then match each of these terms with its definition.

Let's not cheese off American authorities. Just in case it is a fantasy of yours to get trapped in a cheese factory for a night in South Dakota and in Tennessee, bad news: it's illegal to fall asleep in a cheese factory there. In the dairy state of Wisconsin, it's illegal to make baby Swiss cheese – a kind of Gruyère – if you do not have 'well-developed eyes'. What does this mean? Is the career out of your reach if you're as blind as a bat? Or is it even so if you're just slightly short-sighted and need to wear glasses? That may be pushing the screening process a bit too far, isn't it? Oh, wait a minute… As it happens, the eyes are the name given to the holes forming inside that type of cheese during the maturing. If the cheese does not develop holes big enough to qualify as 'eyes', it cannot be called Swiss cheese.

a. To cheese off
b. out of reach
c. screening process
d. fall asleep
e. short-sighted
f. as blind as a bat

1. myope comme une taupe
2. start sleeping
3. inaccessible
4. unable to see things from far
5. to irritate
6. selection

UNIT 4

22. À l'aide des indices fournis, assemblez les groupes de lettres pour reconstituer ces traductions anglaises (mots employés dans le texte de l'exercice 21).

a. produits laitiers (beurre, fromage, etc.) ....

b. expérience excitante imaginaire ....

c. légèrement ....

d. trou ....

e. site de production ....

SY   RY
SL   FA   ORY
NTA   CT   DAI   FA
     LE   HO   IGH
              TLY

23. Separate the words properly so as to form a meaningful text, and complete the crossword puzzle with words used in the text.

INENGLANDTHEREISSUCHATHINGAS
CHEESEROLLINGCOMPETITIONS-PEOPLE
ROLLAHUGEWHEELOFCHEESEDOWNAHILL
ANDRUNAFTERITINANATTEMPTTOGETIT
FIRST.THEMOSTFAMOUSCHEESE
ROLLINGTAKESPLACEINBROCK
WORTH,WHERETHECHEESEISROLLED
DOWNCOOPERSHILL.INTHESMALLER
VILLAGEOFRANDWICK,THREEWHEELS
OFCHEESEAREROLLEDAROUNDTHE
CHURCH.WHENTHECOMPETITION
ISOVER,THEVILLAGERSALLSNACKON
ONEWHEEL.THELEGENDSAYSTHATS
HARINGITWILLBRINGPROTECTION
TOTHEVILLAGE.

Across

2. en-cas

3. colline

4. tentative

5. meule

Down

1. rime avec *sausage*

2. partager

43

UNIT 4

24. À l'aide des traductions françaises fournies, reconstituez ces noms loufoques de fromages anglais en reliant chaque chiffre à une lettre.

- **a.** Stinking
- **b.** Tickle
- **c.** Fat
- **d.** Timber
- **e.** Dirt
- **f.** Drunken

- **1.** Lover
- **2.** Hooligan
- **3.** more (one word)
- **4.** Bishop
- **5.** doodle (one word)
- **6.** Bottom Girl

Indices : évêque puant, chatouille encore, la fille aux grosses fesses, gribouillage sur bois, amateur de poussière/saleté, agitateur ivre

26. Entourez la bonne préposition dans les reformulations de la partie en rouge de ce proverbe allemand.

If you don't want to be hung yourself, blame the dog for stealing the sausage.

a. put the blame *on/off/of* the dog
b. accuse the dog *from/for/of* stealing
c. hold the dog responsible *of/on/for* stealing

25. En changeant les lettres en gras dans les mots en majuscules de ces citations, vous découvrirez un proverbe.

a. 'It is better to eat bread with love than fowl with **B**RIEF ....'. (Bolivian proverb).
Tip: chagrin

b. 'An appetite is a true companion to PLAI**T** .... bread'. (Sicilian proverb).
Tip: means 'basic'

c. 'Eat leeks in March and wild garlic in May, and all year after PHYSICI**ST**s .... may play'. (Welsh proverb.)
Tip: means 'doctor'

27. Entourez la bonne proposition.
a. A(n) *Scottish/Welsh/Irish* uncle is your mother's or father's first cousin.
b. Going *Dutch/Welsh/Irish* at the restaurant means that you share the bill.
c. To *Scottish/French/Welsh* on someone means not to repay them a debt.

UNIT 4

28. Devinez le verbe qui a été effacé dans cette citation du comédien irlandais Dylan Moran, sachant qu'il est synonyme de la proposition **a.** Que signifie ce *phrasal verb* ?

> *Cooking? Oh we were great, you'd take anything and melt cheese on it, and the one who could guess what it was didn't have to .... up!*

a. do the dishes
b. do the laundry
c. do the ironing

29. En résolvant ces trois petites devinettes de manière successive, vous trouverez le mot manquant dans cette autre citation de Dylan Moran (tip: he thinks that eggs smell really bad).

> *Eggs! They're not a food; they belong in no group! They're just ....s clothed in substance!*

a. sombre : _ a _ k
→ change the last letter and you get
b. fléchette : _ a _ _
→ change the first letter and you're there
c. _ a _ _

END-OF-CHAPTER TEST

30. Translate these sentences into English.

1. J'étais en train de préparer de la chapelure avec le pain rassis quand je me suis souvenu qu'il me fallait de la muscade pour la recette.

....
....
....

2. Pas étonnant que tes parents n'aient pas aimé ta recette avec un fromage fort. Ils ne mangent plus de produits laitiers depuis dix ans.

....
....

3. C'est la deuxième fois que je prépare une omelette aux poireaux cette semaine. Je pouvais cuisiner gallois quand j'étais jeune.

....
....

4. Il m'avait donné ce conseil : ajouter deux jaunes d'œuf et un morceau de fromage friable.

....
....
....

5. Ces informations sur la cuisine galloise me paraissent raisonnables.

....
....

45

UNIT 5

Here comes another everyday low-budget yet delightful recipe that will fuel body and soul. When it comes to making baked beans, there are two different approaches to choose from: Boston style and British style. On the one hand, Boston is said to be the town of origin of baked beans, hence its nickname, 'Bean Town'. On the other hand, the British are also fond of baked beans, which are still the top-selling convenience food staple in the United Kingdom. The Boston version is a dish consisting of white beans cooked in tomato, bacon or salt pork, and molasses, baked for at least six hours. The British version is altogether different insofar as it is meatless, contains little to no sugar, is stewed rather than baked, and is bound in a sauce that is not as thick as the one in the American version. Our recipe is going to be the British one. The British typically consume baked beans with bangers and mash, fried eggs, or simply on toast, in a snacky dish aptly named 'beans on toast'. Besides, baked beans are also part and parcel of a hearty English fry-up. If you are to go British all the way, put the kettle on and have a 'cuppa' builder's tea – strong tannic black tea, such as Assam, brewed for about four minutes and served with a nice splash of milk and two sugars!

BAKED BEANS

INGREDIENTS

6 SERVINGS:
- 500 g of dried haricots or white beans
- 2 carrots, peeled and chopped
- 1 stick of celery, chopped
- 500 g of tinned tomatoes, chopped
- 3 tablespoons of tomato ketchup
- 3 tablespoons of olive oil
- 3 garlic cloves, crushed
- 1 teaspoon of flour
- 350 ml of water
- salt and pepper, to taste

1. Soak the beans in cold water overnight (recommended to avoid getting an upset stomach and bloating).

2. The following day, drain and wash the beans. Put them in a pot, cover with cold water, and cook until tender (about 90 minutes). It is tempting to use canned white beans instead if you're in a rush, but they usually collapse into a mush, so it may not be worth rushing things and spoiling the dish.

3. Now the sauce. Fry the celery, carrots, and garlic in a pan with some oil until tender.

4. Add the tomatoes and the ketchup, and stir well. Leave to simmer until you get a smooth texture.

5. Add the flour and the glass of water, and stir well. Salt and pepper according to taste.

6. Add the beans and let simmer for about 20 minutes.

UNIT 5

QUESTIONS AROUND THE TEXT

1. Tell if these statements are right or wrong.   RIGHT   WRONG

a. Baked beans originate from Great Britain.
b. The Boston and the British bean recipes are only slightly different.
c. The British version is devoid of meat and comes in a thinner sauce.
d. The British hardly ever enjoy baked beans these days.
e. Baked beans are a versatile food.
f. Soaking the beans overnight prevents them from getting all mushy.

2. Remettez les lettres dans l'ordre pour former la traduction anglaise des mots suivants utilisés dans le texte.

a. means *delicious*: THLUGIFEDL ....
b. bean town: NOSBOT ....
c. copieux: YERATH ....
d. alimenter, nourrir: LUFE ....
e. tasse (familier): PACUP ....
f. bouilloire: ELTEKT ....
g. goutte, soupçon: LHASPS ....

3. Complete the following crossword puzzle with words used in the text or in the recipe.

Across
2. lisse, homogène
4. se démonter
5. égoutter

Down
1. gâcher, rater (ici)
2. (faire) tremper
3. pendant la nuit

4. Dites à quoi renvoient les éléments suivants dans le texte.

a. *One* dans *as the one in the American version* (l. 13)

....

b. *Its* dans *hence its nickname 'Bean Town'* (l. 5-6)

....

UNIT 5

5. Fill in the blanks with the following items.

ON THE ONE HAND/ON THE OTHER HAND/THE FORMER/THE LATTER/EVERYDAY/ EVERY DAY/ALTOGETHER/ALL TOGETHER

a. Baked beans are an .... food, but people do not eat them ....

b. The four sisters live ...., although they have .... different personalities.

c. Beans and eggs are British staples. .... are served baked, ... scrambled or fried.

d. .... beans are delicious, ... they can cause gas.

6. Circle the correct proposition.

a. 'Saucisses-purée' (familier) are:
   1. 'English fry-up'
   2. 'bangers and mash'
   3. 'beans on toast'

b. 'Part and parcel' (l. 17) means:
   1. essential to
   2. to be avoided
   3. optional in

c. A 'fry-up' (l. 18) is:
   1. a dish composed of leftovers
   2. a full English breakfast
   3. a sunny-side-up egg

d. I'll 'put the kettle on' (l. 18-19) is a phrase British people say when:
   1. they've had breakfast
   2. they are going to make some tea
   3. they sneeze

e. If you are 'in a rush' (recette, 2.), you need to:
   1. make up
   2. give up
   3. hurry up

f. You are 'aptly named' (l. 16) if a name:
   1. upsets you
   2. suits you
   3. makes you laugh

7. Les mots de liaison suivants sont placés dans la mauvaise phrase, remettez-les dans la phrase qui convient.

a. Baked beans are tasty. *yet* → ...., everybody loves them.

b. *hence* → .... beans can cause gas, it is generally advised to soak them before cooking them.

c. I have cooked my beans without soaking them, *insofar as* → .... the bloating now.

d. Baked beans are very inexpensive, *besides* → .... even richer people love them.

8. Place the following words in the right sentences.

PAINFUL/SORE/UPSET

a. When you get a(n) .... stomach, you have a stomach ache.

b. Toothaches can be really ....

c. When your throat hurts, you have a(n) .... throat.

UNIT 5

9. Placez les préfixes *un-*, *dis-*, *mis-*, *under-* et *over-* au bon endroit.

It is ……….fair to say beans are bad; they are part of a healthy diet, and they are largely ……….estimated as a high-fiber beneficial food for instance. The thing is, there is a ……….understanding about them. Doctor's ……….approval of beans is often based on the high sodium content of canned beans. The digestive problems they can cause is also ……….estimated as they will not cause so much gas if cooked properly.

12. Bring the necessary modifications to the second sentence.

a. I usually **choose** tomatoes from the market.
→ Yesterday I ……………… tomatoes from my garden.

b. Beans are **bound** in a sauce.
→ I always ……………… my beans in a sauce.

c. There is **very little to no** meat in the dish.
→ There are **very** ……………… **to no** sausages in it.

d. The **slices of bread** are good.
→ The toast ……………… good.

13. Placez chaque indicateur de quantité individuelle à côté du nom qui lui correspond.
LUMP/BUNCH/STICK/PINCH/PLATE/MUG/CAN/CHUNK OR SIDE/SLICE/CARTON

a. a ……………… of baked beans
b. a ……………… of toast
c. a ……………… of sugar
d. a ……………… of salt
e. a ……………… of mash
f. a ……………… of tea
g. a ……………… of milk
h. a ……………… of bacon
i. a ……………… of carrots
j. a ……………… of celery

10. Trouvez les deux adjectifs composés, utilisés dans le texte, synonymes de ces reformulations.

a. that sells very well: ……………………… (l. ……….)
b. budget-friendly: ……………………… (l. ……….)

11. Dites quelle seule et même préposition manque dans toutes ces phrases.

The demand for economical recipes is ……………… the rise – beans can be the answer. They are useful indeed when you need to cook ……………… a budget. Unless you are ……………… a special diet, you can have them ……………… a daily basis. I had ……………… my mind to cook real Boston beans for you. Could you come over at my place at seven ……………… the dot ……………… Saturday?

14. Correct the verbal structures that are wrong.

Sorry I didn't hear you call. I was too busy discuss our meal with the children. They asked me to make beans on toast again. I don't really like them, as you know. They make me farting. But doctors say that consuming beans once a week is good for you, so I ended up saying 'all right.' But rather than to wait for a night – I didn't feel like cooking all morning to be honest – I preferred to use tinned beans. Well I regret to do that as they turned into mush. There's no arguing homemade ones are the best, and everybody can afford to making baked beans. I also understand why your friend from Boston can't stand eating British-style beans. But using molasses in beans is far from be common in the U.K. Next time you're both around though, let me bake a good batch of Boston beans for you two.

15. Reliez chaque début de phrase à sa suite.

a. He really misses
b. Remember to buy
c. Why not
d. I got her
e. What's the point of
f. It was a pleasure

1. to try this authentic Boston recipe.
2. to change the recipe.
3. soaking your beans when you can buy tinned ones?
4. use tinned beans?
5. tasting the one his mother makes.
6. the ketchup for the beans tomorrow.

16. Mettez les verbes entre parenthèses à la forme verbale *to*, *-ing* ou Ø.

a. Help me .... *(make)* the proper Boston recipe.
b. Be careful .... *(use)* just a little garlic.
c. You were right .... *(buy)* dried beans.
d. Go on .... *(cook)*, don't mind me.

17. Reformulez en fondant ces deux phrases en une seule phrase commençant par un gérondif (verbe en *-ing*).

He wants to try the full English breakfast. It is a good idea.

UNIT 5

18. Tell if these statements are right or wrong.

RIGHT   WRONG

a. *Latter* et *later* se prononcent de la même façon.

b. *Tomato* se prononce [t^eu'mat^euou] en américain et [t^eu'mèït^euou] en anglais.

c. *Soak* rime avec *joke*.

d. *Baked* rime avec *naked*.

19. Placez chacun de ces mots selon la prononciation de sa graphie *ea*.

LEAST/HEARTY/INSTEAD

a. [â] ....

b. [è] ....

c. [i] ....

20. Chassez l'intrus.

USUALLY/DECISION/TREASURE/ASIA/SUGAR/LEISURE/CASUAL/VISUAL/OCCASION

21. Classez ces mots dans le tableau selon la prononciation de leur *ch*.

CHARACTER/CHALET/ORCHESTRA/ARCHITECT/CHAOS/PSYCHOLOGY/MOUSTACHE/CHAUFFEUR/APPROACH/STOMACH/MONARCH/PSYCHE/CHEMISTRY/MECHANIC/CHOOSE/CHIC/MACHINE/CHOPPED

[TCH]	[K]	[CH]

22. Soulignez les mots qui sont accentués dans les phrases suivantes (cela signifie qu'on les prononce plus fort que les autres).

a. The full breakfast with bacon and eggs is filling.

b. Did you leave your cup of tea on the table?

c. Beans on toast is not a staple in Germany.

d. I forgive them, but I don't forgive you.

UNIT 5

VOCABULARY INTERLUDE

23. Circle the right proposition to solve this riddle.
I am used in chilli con carne, I am…

a. the chickpea   b. the kidney bean   c. the French bean

24. Circle the food category dry beans belong to.
PULSES/CITRUS/SQUASH

25. Reliez chaque expression à sa signification.

a. Tomayto, tomahto.
b. What does that have to do with the price of tea in China?
c. To be the toast of (the town)
d. To be a bean counter

1. To try by all means not to spend money.
2. Unimportant difference.
3. To be famous and loved in a certain place.
4. That's irrelevant.

26. Complete the blanks with either *tea*, *bean* or *kettle*.

a. I like my cousin but his sister is another .... of fish.
b. Don't ask me about computers, I don't know ....s about those.
c. I love my job. I would not quit for all the .... in China.
d. I know about your little secret. Your wife has spilt the ....s.
e. .... and sympathy is the least you could offer a friend in need.

27. Placez chaque mot dérivé de *bean* à côté de sa définition.
BEANIE/BEANBAG/JELLYBEAN

a. pouf (siège)   ....
b. bonbon « haricot »   ....
c. bonnet   ....

28. Placez ces mots au bon endroit pour reconstituer le surnom des villes suivantes.
MOTOR/APPLE/SIN/WIND/EMERALD/~~BEAN~~/EASY

a. Boston is **Bean** Town.
b. Las Vegas is .... City.
c. Chicago is The ....y City.
d. New Orleans is The Big ....
e. Detroit is .... City.
f. Seattle is .... City.
g. New York is The Big ....

UNIT 5

BACK TO WORK – LAUGH AND LEARN

And now let us close this unit with great delicacy. As you know, beans are a potential source of social embarrassment as they make people fart – in Florida by the way, it is not allowed to fart in public places after 6 p.m. Fart jokes with baked beans are a classic of bathroom humour, particularly popular with teenagers. A children's song in the U.K. goes 'Beans, beans, are good for your heart/The more you eat, the more you fart'. The fart vocabulary is rich: you *break wind* or *pass gas* if you're being formal, you *cut a fart* (or *an air biscuit*), you *cut the cheese* or you *toot* if you're in a more familiar register. But the vocabulary of the fart expands to things beyond our digestive system: *to fart around* means 'to waste time doing nothing', and an *old fart* is an older person with old-fashioned ideas. Finally, a temporary loss of memory or a silly mistake is a *brain fart*!

29. Trouvez les mots du texte ci-dessus auxquels ces indices font allusion.

a. type of humour about bodily functions: ....
b. food metaphors used to refer to farts: .... and ....
c. means « glander » ....
d. means « vieux schnock » ....
e. means « un trou de mémoire » ....
f. Changez une lettre à *paste* et je serai l'homonyme du mot signifiant « taille » ; je signifie « gâcher ». ....
g. Changez une lettre à *foot* et je signifierai à la fois « péter » ou « klaxonner ». ....
h. Mon *u* ne se prononce pas. Je suis apprécié à l'heure du thé. ....

30. Reformulez ces citations à l'aide des schémas de phrases fournis.

a. 'Eat beans for lunch and have no friends at the dinner table.' (Greek proverb)
→ Eat beans .... lunchtime and do not have .... friends at the dinner table.

b. 'Every man knows the smell of his own fart.' (Confucius)
→ All .... the smell of ....

c. 'If man has no tea in him, he is incapable of understanding truth and beauty.' (Japanese proverb)
→ If man has no tea in him, he is unable .... truth and beauty.

d. 'I would rather have a cup of tea than sex.' (Boy George)
→ I would prefer a cup of tea .... sex.

UNIT 5

31. Remettez les lettres des mots en majuscules dans l'ordre pour reconstituer une citation correcte (indice entre parenthèses).

a. 'Drinking a daily cup of tea will surely VETRAS *(to die of hunger)* .... the apothecary.' (Chinese proverb)

b. 'Who SAREF *(is afraid of)* .... laughing will die of fart.' (Estonian proverb)

c. 'The ill NIWD *(current of air)* .... that blows is probably your mother-in-law farting.' (Polish proverb)

32. Circle the correct proposition.

a. 'Three comforts of old age: fire, tea, and *tobacco/tabacco/tobocco*.' (Welsh proverb)

b. 'To disappear like a fart in Sahara' is a Finnish proverb which means *s'évaporer*, un équivalent anglais pourrait être :

    1. To vanish into thin air.

    2. Absence makes the heart grow fonder.

END-OF-CHAPTER TEST

33. Translate these sentences into English.

1. Je prépare les authentiques *baked beans* de Boston depuis quelques années. J'utilise un peu de mélasse dans ma recette et j'ajoute une bonne dose de vinaigre. Je ne mangerais la recette anglaise pour rien au monde !

2. Les étudiants ne peuvent pas se permettre de préparer des plats trop onéreux. Les haricots sont pratiques quand on a un budget serré et qu'on n'a pas envie de cuisiner.

3. D'un côté, j'aime le petit déjeuner anglais avec son pain grillé et ses œufs sur le plat, mais, de l'autre, je déteste le thé noir. Je préfère le thé vert, dont le goût est complètement différent.

4. Les enfants préfèrent la sauce sucrée et épaisse des haricots de Boston à la recette britannique, en particulier avec leur saucisse-purée. Peux-tu m'aider à éplucher les pommes de terre ? Je suis occupée à frire les saucisses.

5. Mon oncle Ted est un vieux schnock. Il a renoncé à manger des haricots car il dit que ça donne mal au ventre.

UNIT 6

Our next recipe has been an undisputed mainstay of British diet for decades, in households as well as in pubs. Perfect on a cold winter's night, this ultimate comfort food dish suits any occasion and is given the thumbs up across age and social barriers – it is particularly popular with children. Shepherd's pie is a northern dish of humble rural origin, the British equivalent of our French hachis parmentier, as it were. It layers mashed potato with a filling of mince cooked with vegetables (generally carrots, celery, peas, and tomato paste), with a cheddar cheese crust top. For a long time, this dish was just a way to use up leftovers. In the United Kingdom, it is called *shepherd's pie* if the meat used is lamb and *cottage pie* if you are using beef. The Irish tend to favour the use of lamb. Regardless, it is usually consumed with a side of carrots and peas. Some people now experiment with the original recipe, using turnips, parsnips, sweet potatoes, or squash – the family pumpkin belongs to – in healthier and lighter alternatives to the mashed potato. Now, one question remains: what beverage can you pair it with? If Britons would see nothing out of the ordinary washing it down with a cup of tea, a stout or a glass of red wine may be more appealing to most Frenchies. For a non-alcoholic option, try iced tea or sparkling water.

SHEPHERD'S PIE

INGREDIENTS

4 SERVINGS:

- 3 tablespoons of olive oil
- 2 onions, chopped
- 3 carrots, peeled and chopped
- 2 celery sticks, chopped
- 2 tablespoons of tomato paste
- 500 g of mince (beef or lamb)
- 2 tablespoons of flour
- 400 ml of beef stock
- 2 tablespoons of Worcestershire sauce
- 1 bay leaf
- 5 big potatoes, peeled and cut into chunks
- 50 g of butter (plus 20 g, optional)
- 125 ml of milk
- 100 g of sharp cheddar, grated
- salt and pepper, to taste

1. Heat the oil in a large saucepan. Add the onions, the carrots, and the celery, and cook until soft. Then add the mince and cook for a few minutes, stirring, until the meat changes colour.

2. Add the flour and cook, stirring until combined. Add the tomato paste, the Worcestershire sauce, and the bay leaf, and fry for a few minutes. Pour over the stock. Bring to a simmer on low heat for about 30 minutes, stirring occasionally. Season with salt and pepper.

3. Meanwhile, heat the oven to 180° C. Then prepare the mash: boil the potatoes in salted water for 10-15 mins until tender and drain. Mash the potatoes until smooth. Add the butter and the milk and stir well, until combined. Season with salt and pepper.

4. Put the meat mixture in a baking dish and top with the mash and the grated cheese. You can add a few knobs of butter to top it all. Bake for 20 to 25 minutes, until the top is brown.

UNIT 6

QUESTIONS AROUND THE TEXT

1. Fill in the blanks with the words from the list provided below.
TOP/CHEESE/COMPANION/SPEAK/WARMING/MASHABLE/INSTEAD/
COTTAGE/CLASSIC/UPS/DIETING/COUNTRYSIDE/POTATOES/DARK/
EMBRACED

Shepherd's pie is like a hachis parmentier, so to .... This .... dish has long been a .... in the U.K, where the dish is .... by everyone, rich and poor, children as well as grown-............................ It is a .... dish coming from the North, composed of mashed .... with mince lamb, various vegetables and .... on the .... It's called .... *pie* and not *shepherd's pie* when beef is used .... of lamb. For health and .... reasons, some people now replace the potatoes with other .... vegetables. .... beer is a nice .... to the dish.

2. Tell if these statements are right or wrong.

	RIGHT	WRONG
a. Squash is a type of pumpkin.		
b. Most British people think that drinking tea with shepherd's pie is abnormal.		
c. For a long time, the dish was a way not to waste the heat from ovens after baking.		
d. Kids really enjoy shepherd's pie.		
e. The meat stock is added right at the end of the recipe.		

L	D	C	B	T	S	Q	D	D	I	E	T
V	E	O	D	B	U	T	U	G	F	B	C
T	N	F	Y	G	V	R	O	O	M	F	D
K	Q	K	T	K	G	I	N	A	X	L	R
B	U	M	G	O	A	F	L	I	O	B	N
T	U	O	I	V	V	L	O	H	P	E	O
S	J	D	G	N	S	E	E	B	N	E	U
Q	S	Y	S	T	C	S	R	U	W	F	O
U	T	X	U	I	U	E	Z	S	O	Q	Q
A	A	S	O	O	V	E	U	R	N	N	N
S	P	K	H	W	M	S	T	O	C	K	S
H	D	L	P	P	A	R	S	N	I	P	J

3. Find the English translations of these words in the following grid (words used in the text or the recipe).

a. foyer ....
b. viande de bœuf ....
c. courge(s) ....
d. navet ....
e. régime alimentaire ....
f. viande d'agneau ....
g. restes de repas ....
h. panais ....
i. viande hachée ....
j. bouillon ....
k. noisette (de beurre) ....

UNIT 6

4. Les mots en gras (issus du texte) ont été placés dans la mauvaise phrase. Remettez-les dans celle qui leur convient.

a. A **stout** → .... is a period of ten years.

b. The **beverage** → .... is popular at Halloween time.

c. A **pumpkin** → .... is a person who keeps sheep.

d. Coffee is a **shepherd** → ...., as well as fruit juice or water.

e. A **sparkling water** → .... is a type of dark beer like Guinness.

f. **decade** → .... contains bubbles of gas.

5. Correct the mistakes in these rephrasings.

a. *To wash up* means *to drink something after putting food in your mouth*.

....
....

b. *To give something the thumbs up* (l. 4) means *to give it your disapproval*.

....
....

c. *As it were* (l. 7) means *in a way, but not completely, not one hundreds per cents*.

....
....

d. The word *mince* is British; its American equivalent is *grinded beef*.

....
....

e. An *undisputed* (l. 1) *matter* is a matter everybody *agrees of*.

....
....

f. *Regardless* (l. 13) means *in some cases* here.

....

6. *Mincemeat* est un faux ami (le *mincemeat* ne contient pas de viande). De quoi s'agit-il ?

a. d'un filtre à thé

b. d'une pince à toast

c. d'un petit gâteau fourré aux fruits

7. Indiquez la marque du *génitif* (souvent utilisé pour traduire la possession).

a. Rufus......... parents are Irish.

b. My parents......... parents were Scottish.

c. A hot summer......... night.

d. Jack......... and Donna......... kids are twins.

e. Their children......... favourite dish is mash.

8. Circle the correct proposition.

a. If I .... not .... a vegetarian, I would try your shepherd's pie.

   1. had … been   **2.** was – Ø   **3.** were – Ø

b. I would have come if you .... me.

   1. had invited

   2. would have invited

   3. invited

c. It's high time you ....

   1. had left   **2.** left   **3.** leave

d. You .... better put more mince in it.

   1. should   **2.** would   **3.** had

e. The potatoes are tender. Maybe you .... drain them.

   1. should   **2.** need   **3.** would

f. I .... I could be with you.

   1. would wish   **2.** wished   **3.** wish

UNIT 6

9. Match the beginning of each sentence with its end.

a. They wish they

b. It has crossed my mind to use turnips instead of potatoes but it

c. People ought to

d. I'd rather

e. I suck at cooking. If only I

f. You should have

1. knew how to cook like you!
2. you didn't smoke in the house.
3. wouldn't have been the same thing.
4. told me you were allergic to onions.
5. use up leftovers and not waste food.
6. had bought more mince!

10. Complétez ce dialogue.

– You used lamb in the pie and I hate it!
– I did not know that. Why didn't you tell me? I .... beef instead if you .... me.

11. Complete the rephrasings of this sentence expressing advice: *'You shouldn't smoke so much.'*

a. You .... better .... so much.

b. .... I were you, I .... not smoke so much.

c. I would advise you .... so much.

12. Corrigez les mots anglais mal orthographiés.

ADRESS/CAROTT/MIROR/ENEMY/ LITTERATURE/ACCROSS/BEGINING/ EXAMPLE/ABRICOT/LANGAGE/ SYROP/FONCTION/PRONUNCIATION/ TO PRONOUNCE/AGGRESSIVE/ TO ACHIEVE/ACCOMMODATION/ EMBARRASSING/TO LOOSE/SEPARATE/ NECESSARY/RHYTHM/DILEMA

13. Rephrase the sentence below, using *whereas* instead of *unlike*.

Unlike the British, who say 'mince,' Americans say 'ground beef.'

14. Entourez les mots dans lesquels le *b* ne se prononce pas.

LAMB/CRUMB/VEGETABLES/HUMBLE/ CLIMB/COMBINED/PLUMBER/THUMB/KNOB

UNIT 6

15. Classez ces mots selon le nombre de fois où l'on entend le son *[i]* ou *[ɪ]* dans leur prononciation.

COTTAGE/MINCE/RECIPE/PARTICULARLY/KIND/MINUTE/EQUIVALENT/FILLING/CELERY/BISCUIT/EXPERIMENT/ORIGINAL/BEVERAGE/COMPLETE/KNOWLEDGE/WOMEN/LIE/BUSINESS/SECRET/MEDIA/PRIVATE/IDEAL/GENE/STIR

0	
1	
2	
3	

16. Pick out the statements that are correct.

a. *Stout* rime avec *out*.
b. *Minute* se prononce ['miniout].
c. *Worcestershire* se prononce ['wout**eu**sh^{eu}].
d. *Cottage* rime avec *page*.
e. *Squash* rime avec *spinach*.
f. *Mince* se prononce comme *mints* (menthes).

17. Entourez l'intrus dans ces mots contenant tous la graphie *ea*.

PEA/MEAT/LEAF/HEAT/HEALTHIER/TEA/APPEALING/SEASON/MEANWHILE

18. Transformez chaque mot en un homophone en lui ajoutant ou en lui retirant une lettre.

a. night (l. 3): ....
b. wine (l. 20): ....
c. pie: ....

19. Entourez le nombre de syllabes que l'on entend dans les mots suivants.

a. vegetables: 2 – 3 – 4
b. generally: 2 – 3 – 4
c. celery: 2 – 3 – 4
d. usually: 2 – 3 – 4

UNIT 6

20. Entourez la bonne proposition.

a. Le *u* dans *butter*, *ultimate*, *thumb*, *humble*, *crust*, *just*, *pumpkin*, *cup* se prononce :

   1. [eu]   2. [eu]   3. [iou]

b. *Diet* se prononce :

   1. ['daït]   2. ['daïeut]   3. ['dieut]

c. *Beverage* se prononce :

   1. ['bèvridj]   2. ['beuveuridj]   3. ['bèvrèïdj]

21. Indiquez l'accent de mot dans les termes suivants en mettant un ' avant la syllabe qu'on entend plus que les autres.

a. perfect   **k.** trainee
b. hello   **l.** winter
c. carrot   **m.** abroad
d. sparkling   **n.** shepherd
e. turnip   **o.** July
f. cartoon   **p.** mutton
g. Chinese   **q.** butter
h. decade   **r.** cottage
i. comfort   **s.** enough
j. across   **t.** unreal

VOCABULARY INTERLUDE

22. Find the missing letters.

a. Meat from a young cow: __ EA __
b. Meat from older sheep: __U __TON

23. En prenant la première lettre de ces mots à deviner, vous trouverez le mot correspondant à la définition fournie en dessous.

a. not a boy: _ _ _ _
b. not poor at all: _ _ _ _
c. opposite of below: _ _ _ _
d. animal's doctor: _ _ _
e. not old: _ _ _ _

.... is a sauce made from the juice of meat.

24. Classez ces adjectifs du plus cuit au moins cuit.

UNDERDONE/OVERDONE/RARE/RAW/MEDIUM/WELL-DONE

++ ....

.... - -

25. Classez ces types de lait du plus gras au moins gras et entourez l'équivalent de « lait écrémé ».

SEMI-SKIMMED/SKIMMED/WHOLE

++ ....

.... - -

UNIT 6

26. Entourez la pièce d'agneau qui s'est glissée dans cette liste de pièces de bœuf.

rib-eye

chop

sirloin

T-bone

27. Trouvez les lettres manquantes dans ces noms de fromages anglais très populaires.

a. __hed__a__

b. S__ilto__

c. Shro__ __hire

28. Circle the correct proposition.

a. The right translation for *fromage de chèvre* is:
1. goat milk cheese
2. goat milk's cheese
3. goat's milk cheese

b. *Soft cheese* is:
1. du fromage à pâte molle
2. du bleu
3. du fromage fondu

c. Le *fromage frais* is:
1. cottage cheese
2. clotted cream
3. custard

d. *Cream cheese* is:
1. fromage blanc
2. fromage frais
3. fromage fondu

e. *Swiss cheese* is a type of cheese French people call:
1. camembert
2. gruyère
3. feta

29. Fill in the blanks with either *ox* or *ewe*.

a. 'Cheese from the .... *(female sheep)*, milk from the goat, butter from the cow'.
(Spanish proverb)

b. 'The end of an .... *(male cow)* is beef, and the end of a lie is grief'.
(Malagasi proverb)

30. Complétez les espaces par *beef*, *mince* ou *meat* dans ces expressions idiomatiques.

a. I have a .... with my boss. We had an argument yesterday.

b. This restaurant offers very basic dishes. It's very '.......................... and two veg.'

c. This chapter is crucial; it is the .... and potatoes of the story.

d. Steven is stupid, as thick as ....

e. Your essay is too short. You need to .... it up with a few arguments.

63

UNIT 6

31. Reliez chaque début de phrase à l'expression idiomatique lui correspondant.

a. The mayor is an important person; he's
b. Tim is a really nice guy; he's
c. This meeting is important; it's
d. The company needs some action now;
e. This restaurant is so good it doesn't need advertising;

1. as gentle as a lamb.
2. fine words butter no parsnips.
3. a big cheese.
4. good wine needs no bush.
5. not small potatoes.

32. À partir de cet échange, déduisez le sens de l'expression en rouge, puis entourez les deux expressions qui expriment la même idée parmi les propositions a. à d.

Boss: – I need this file completed right now!

Personal assistant: – Yes, boss. I'll do it in two shakes of a lamb's tail!

a. before you can say Jack Robinson
b. in a pig's eye
c. on a roll
d. in the blink of an eye

Signifie : ....

33. Circle the proverb that means 'To be surrounded by things you cannot make use of.'

a. To need Dutch courage
b. Life is not all beer and skittles
c. Water, water everywhere and not a drop to drink

34. Placez chacun de ces termes au bon endroit.

DRINKING/SPARKLING/HOLY/RUNNING/SPRING/STILL/TAP

a. eau du robinet : .... water
b. eau plate : .... water
c. eau bénite : .... water
d. eau courante : .... water
e. eau gazeuse : .... water
f. eau de source : .... water
g. eau potable : .... water

35. Fill in the blanks with *beer, tea, water,* or *wine*.

a. Something is '........................ under the bridge' when it has happened and cannot be changed.
b. If you have champagne taste on a .... budget, you like things you cannot afford.
c. 'Not for all the .... in China' is the English equivalent of 'pour rien au monde'.
d. When you invite a date to the restaurant, you .... and dine him or her.
e. If you are in deep ...., you are in a difficult situation.

UNIT 6

BACK TO WORK – LAUGH AND LEARN

The British love spending time in pubs, just to meet their friends and have a drink, play darts, or grab a bite – Shepherd's pie is a classic pub dish. Most pubs have traditional names like *The Black Swan* or *The Red Lion*, but some have funny ones like *The Bunch of Carrots* (Hereford), *The Drunken Duck* (Ambleside), *The Dirty Duck* (Coventry), *The Goat and Tricycle* (Bournemouth), *The Goat and Compasses* (Hull), *The Idle Cook* (Bradford), *The Cow and Snuffers* (Cardiff, Wales), *The Moody Cow* (Upton Bishop), *The Snooty Fox* (Lowick), *The Bucket of Blood* (Hayle), *My Father's Moustache* (Lincolnshire), and *The Jolly Taxpayer* (Portsmouth).

36. Trouvez à quels pubs mentionnés dans le texte ci-dessus font référence les devinettes suivantes.

a. Rabbits' favourite pub: ....
b. Cheerful citizen: ....
c. Tobacco cattle: ....
d. Quack quack pubs: .... and ....
e. Caprine GPS system: ....
f. Meh-eh-eh-eh bike: ....
g. Arrogant Reynard: ....
h. Lazy chef: ....
i. My old man's mouth brow: ....
j. Temperamental ruminant: ....
k. Serial killers' pub: ....

UNIT 6

37. **Placez le bon numéro de plat dans le texte qui suit.**

a. fruits secs enrobés de bacon

b. type de dessert compact et dense contenant des fruits secs

c. plat composé de restes, son nom vient du bruit qu'il produit quand on le prépare

d. dessert contenant de la crème fouettée et des fraises

e. saucisse entourée de pâte à Yorkshire pudding

Pubs are not the only things with funny names in Great Britain. Some dishes have surprising names as well. We have already alluded to *bangers and mash* in a previous chapter. There is also *bubble and squeak* for instance (….), the toad in the hole (….) devils on horseback (….), Eton mess (….), and spotted dick (….), which has nothing to do with a male attribute affected by some sexual disease. Speaking of which, you'd better be careful with the phrase *Meat and two veg* because in slang 'meat' means 'penis', so you get the idea…

38. **Find the missing letters in the words in capital characters (clues in brackets).**

a. 'Beer before wine, you'll feel _INE *(all right)*. Wine before beer, you'll feel QUE_ _ *(strange, weird)*.' (English proverb)

b. 'Wine is the best broom for T_OU_LE *(problems)*.' (Japanese proverb)

c. 'Old wine and friends IM_ _OVE *(get better)* with age.' (Italian proverb)

d. 'A home without G_ _STS *(people invited)*, a village without S_EPHE_DS *(sheep keepers)*, both are HOPE_E_S *(without hope)* indeed.' (Kurdish proverb)

39. **Change one letter in the words in bold so as to find the real quote.**

a. 'I **HOOK** → ………………… with wine, and sometimes I even add it to the food.' (W. C. Fields)

b. 'Never touch the **STAFF** → ………………… – very unhealthy. Fish fuck in it.' (W. C. Fields, about water)

40. **Entourez la ou les significations de l'expression en rouge dans ce proverbe espagnol.**

It is better to have bread left over than to run short of wine.

a. not much left

b. too much left

c. little left

d. none left at all

41. **Entourez, parmi les propositions, la forme de possessif correcte dans ce proverbe italien.**

a. mans'

b. men'

c. men's

d. mans's

Wine is old ………… milk.

UNIT 6

END-OF-CHAPTER TEST

42. Translate these sentences into English

1. Pourriez-vous remuer le bouillon de veau et faire mijoter la viande de bœuf ?

....

....

2. Si seulement les enfants d'Angus aimaient les navets et la citrouille, j'aurais pu leur faire une purée, avec une bonne dose de fromage râpé pour rendre le tout plus attrayant, et le tour était joué.

....

....

3. Si tu m'avais dit que tu voulais que je te conduise à la gare cet après-midi, j'aurais pris mon plat avec de l'eau gazeuse et non de la bière brune. J'aurais aimé le savoir avant.

....

....

4. Depuis des décennies, des milliers de foyers anglais ne vivent pour ainsi dire que de purée de pommes de terre et d'un peu de viande hachée.

....

....

5. Si j'étais toi, j'utiliserais les restes de viande de mouton et d'agneau pour préparer un *shepherd's pie*. Il est grand temps que l'on arrête de gâcher tant de nourriture.

....

....

UNIT 7

Now it's time to take a walk on the spicy side. Our next stopover is indeed an invitation to India. Britons' love of curry grew out of the relationship between Britain and India during the Victorian era, when India was a British colony. Queen Victoria herself was apparently very partial to curry. To this day, Indian flavours are still among the top English food preferences – so much so that the beloved curry has been challenging the time-honoured fish and chips as Britons' favourite food. Most British people now consider curry as typically British. There's even a National Curry Week. As far as tikka masala is concerned, the origin of the dish is unclear but it may well have been invented in Britain, adapted to European taste for dishes in sauce by an Indian chef in Glasgow (Scotland). Chicken tikka masala consists of pieces of chicken marinated in a yoghurt-based sauce, then baked in an oven called *tandoor*, and served in a spicy sauce – the masala sauce. Tikka generally contains some meat, cream or yoghurt, coconut cream, and spices, but there are as many recipes as there are cooks! It is served with basmati rice, small flat breads called *naans*, and a variety of minty, spicy, and sweet sauces. Pale ales – or light reds if you'd rather go for some wine – make nice combos with tikka.

CHICKEN TIKKA MASALA

INGREDIENTS

4 SERVINGS: (MILD RECIPE)

To marinate the chicken:
- 4 chicken breasts (skinless)
- 1 pot of plain full-fat yoghurt
- 1 tablespoon of ginger (mashed)
- 3 to 5 garlic cloves (crushed)
- 3 tablespoons of lemon juice
- spices (1 teaspoon of each): salt, paprika, cumin powder, garam masala mix

For the sauce:
- 3 tablespoons of olive oil or butter (ghee is the best option for Indian cooking if you have some in store)
- 2 onions (chopped)
- 2 tablespoons of tomato puree
- 300 g of tomatoes (chopped)
- 1 green chilli (chopped)
- 1 tablespoon of ginger (mashed)
- 3 to 5 garlic cloves (crushed)
- 2 teaspoons of sugar

To add in last step:
- 50 ml of coconut cream
- ½ teaspoon of cardamom powder
- 2 or 3 cloves
- 1 teaspoon of paprika
- 1 teaspoon of garam masala mix
- ½ teaspoon of fenugreek
- ½ teaspoon of cinnamon
- a small bunch of coriander leaves for decoration

1. Mix the marinade ingredients together. Cut the chicken into small pieces and put them into the marinade (all the pieces should be coated). Leave to marinate for at least an hour (the longer the better).

2. Make the sauce: heat the oil or butter in a frying pan and add the onions. Fry until soft and golden brown, stirring regularly. Add in the mashed ginger and crushed garlic and fry for a couple of minutes, stirring. Then add the spices and fry for a minute or so. Add the tomato puree, the tomatoes, and a glass of water. Bring to a simmer. Turn the heat down to medium and cook for about 15 minutes.

3. Meanwhile, heat your grill on high heat. Put the chicken pieces on a baking sheet and grill for 6 to 8 minutes on each side.

4. Puree the sauce until smooth. When the chicken is grilled, return the sauce to the pan. Add the rest of the marinade, the chilli, the sugar, the paprika, the cardamom, the cinnamon and the coconut cream into the sauce.

5. Add the chicken pieces, along with the garam masala mix and the fenugreek. Cook for 10 minutes. Sprinkle the chopped coriander on top.

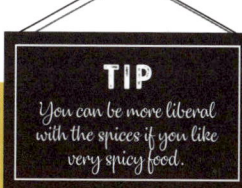

TIP
You can be more liberal with the spices if you like very spicy food.

UNIT 7

QUESTIONS AROUND THE TEXT

1. Tell if these sentences about the text are right or wrong (circle the right letter).

a. British people are mad about curry. W – R
b. The masala sauce is yoghurt-based. W – R
c. Each cook has his or her own masala recipe. W – R
d. India used to be under British power. W – R
e. It is doubtless that tikka masala is a British invention. W – R
f. The recipe given here is a very spicy version. W – R

2. Complete the following crossword puzzle with words used in the text and the recipe.

Across
3. bière blonde (deux mots)
5. sans la peau
7. nature, pour un yaourt
9. blanc (de poulet dans notre contexte, signifie aussi *sein* par ailleurs)
10. clou de girofle
12. lien, rapport entre personnes ou choses
13. abréviation de *combination*

Down
1. much loved
2. signifie *plat* (adjectif) ici, mais peut aussi vouloir dire *appartement*
4. cannelle
6. gingembre
8. ail
11. menthe

UNIT 7

3. Donnez l'orthographe américaine de *favourite* (l. 8) et *flavours* (l. 5).

.................../....................

4. Complétez les espaces par *to* ou *for*.

a. He made an allusion .... your curry recipe.
b. This herb is used .... its minty properties.
c. My addiction .... curry is famous.
d. The recipe .... the sauce is easy.
e. He invited me .... his curry party.
f. The demand .... exotic food is high.
g. The solution .... this problem is complex.
h. The cure .... a broken heart is a good curry.

5. Circle the correct word.

a. This is a cosmopolitan *area/era*. You will find many curry houses in the neighbourhood.
b. All the curry houses are closing down in this city. It is the end of an *area/era*.
c. I can never tell the difference *between/among* curry, garam masala, and paprika.
d. I'm always lost *between/among* spices, I can never tell which is which.
e. It was not *sensible/sensitive* to add so much pepper. You know how *sensible/sensitive* my mother is to spices.

6. Placez les noms fournis ci-dessous à côté du ou des verbes avec lesquels ils s'utilisent.

A RIDE, A FEELING, A PICTURE, A PLAN, AN EXAM, A NAP, FRIENDS, A SEAT, A LAUGH, SHOPPING, POSTED, A MISTAKE, ADVANTAGE, A DOUBT, A PROMISE, YOGA, A DECISION, A BREAK, CARE, A FIGHT, SEX, CALM, FOR A WALK, THE FLU

1. do: ....
2. make: ....
3. take: ....
4. have: ....
5. go: ....
6. keep: ....

7. Trouvez la seule et même préposition qui manque dans toutes les phrases suivantes.

You put in many spices .... purpose! I hate spicy food and you know it! I told you you could cook curry .... condition that it wouldn't be too spicy.
– .... the contrary, my dish was rather underspiced. You're being unfair! You should never eat spices .... an empty stomach anyway!

UNIT 7

8. Circle the names of those who do not like masala.

Emma is partial to it – Henry loathes it – John has a liking for it – Mark is fond of it – Lana has a weakness for it – Ulrich has a soft spot for it – Olivia can't stand it – Ian is keen on it

9. Attribuez chaque trait de caractère à la bonne personne (deux sont non utilisées).

Suzie can't help eating too much tikka. Paula can't wait to try your recipe. Lara can't get enough rice; she could eat some at every meal. Fiona can't stand spices. Erika can't be bothered to cook herself. Tess can't tell the difference between Indian and Pakistani food.

a. She is impatient: ....
b. She is lazy: ....
c. She is clueless: ....
d. She is greedy: ....

10. Remplacez les auxiliaires modaux par l'étiquette indiquant leur probabilité.

1. it is not possible
2. it is possible
3. it is unlikely
4. it is bound to be
5. it is likely (logical)

a. Someone is knocking at the door, it *will be* the takeaway delivery. (n° ....)
b. Mark left home at five, *he should be* here any minute now. (n° ....)
c. The bottle *can't be* empty. I've just opened it. (n° ....)
d. It *might* rain tomorrow, but I really don't think so. (n° ....)
e. The letter *may* arrive a bit late. (n° ....)

11. Ajoutez un pronom réfléchi ou réciproque (*myself*, etc., *each other*, *one another*) si nécessaire.

a. Mike is growing a beard, he no longer shaves ....
b. Make .... at home!
c. My friends and I invite .... every week.
d. They helped .... to curry.
e. We're too tired to go out. We should rest ....
f. Did you enjoy .... at the party?
g. He can't cook for twelve people all by ....
h. Be quiet, she can't concentrate ....
i. They have just met .... and keep kissing .... They love ....

12. Donnez la forme pleine de *'d*, puis proposez une traduction.

a. if you*'d* rather go for (l. 20-21)
....
b. you*'d* better drink beer
....

13. Mettez à la forme négative et interrogative, en utilisant la forme pleine (non contractée).

a. You'd better use much chilli.
....
b. She'd rather add more garlic.
....

14. Dites qui fait le curry le plus épicé et le moins épicé.

Willy's curry is mild – Liam's curry is fiery – Ted's curry is bland – Fiona's curry is piquant

le +: ....
le −: ....

UNIT 7

15. Reliez chaque début de phrase à sa suite.

a. How about
b. If I were you, I
c. Why don't you
d. I would recommend you

1. would add a little curry.
2. adding a little curry?
3. to add a little curry.
4. add a little curry?

16. Remettez les mots dans l'ordre dans ces trois phrases exprimant un conseil, puis attribuez chacune d'elles à la plainte qui lui correspond parmi les énoncés 1-6.

a. manners/ought/respect/table/to/you
....
b. as/doctor/'d/see/as/better/you/possible/soon/a
....
c. a/less/maybe/eat/you/while/for/should
....

1. 'I've put on four pounds.' ....
2. 'I don't know whether I should use more spices or not.' ....
3. 'Burp!' (Peter is belching during lunch) ....
4. 'I'm a bad cook.' ....
5. 'I feel very lonely.' ....
6. 'I've been feeling nauseous lately.' ....

17. Rephrase the following sentence, using *unless* and *if*.

You'd better use coconut cream or your tikka is going to be too dry.

a. ....
b. ....

18. Fill in the blanks with one of these following modals.

WOULD/MUST/NEEDN'T/ABLE TO/MIGHT/COULD/SHOULD

a. You .... cook yourself. We can order instead.
b. They .... / .... have gone easier on the spices. They know we don't like it spicy!
c. When I worked in London, I .... cook curry very well, but this time I'm afraid I was not .... cook decent masala.
d. What time is it? The sun is down. It .... be around ten, right?
e. That's typical, the car .... break down when we need it!

19. Reformulez à l'aide de l'auxiliaire modal approprié (le même dans les deux phrases).

a. You don't have to use much coriander.
....
b. Is it necessary that I bring some chilli?
....

UNIT 7

20. Circle the correct proposition(s).

a. I have got a stomach ache. I need to cut *back on/ back up/back off* spices.

b. My husband's cholesterol is high. He needs to *keep off/keep up/keep out* butter.

c. There are *more and more/fewer and fewer/ less and less* curry houses in town.

d. I love Indian food all the *best/much/more* as it is quite easy to prepare.

e. I have made some masala. Do you want *little/ any/some*? Of course you do!

f. The *less/fewer/lesser* chilli you use, the *milder/more mild/mildest* your dish will be.

21. Circle the correct article (tip: prononcez à haute voix).

a. *a/an* honoured man

b. Tikka is partly *a/an* European dish.

22. Trouvez les homophones de ces mots utilisés dans le texte, auxquels font allusion les devinettes suivantes.

a. I'm the homophone of *week* and I'm not strong. ....

b. I'm the homophone of *plain* and I'm a huge metal bird. ....

c. I'm the homophone of *chilli* and I'm not so warm. ....

23. Entourez l'intrus (prononciation).
WALK/CHALK/BULK/FOLK/ HALF/CALM

24. Entourez les mots dont le *i* se prononce [aï] et soulignez ceux dont il se prononce [i].
MILD/MINUTES /GRILLED/RICE/SPICY/ MINTY/SIDE/LIBERAL/WINE

25. Placez ces mots selon la prononciation de leur graphie *ea*.
UNCLEAR/BREASTS/BREADS/EUROPEAN

a. [i^{eu}] ....
b. [è] ....

26. Entourez les mots dans lesquels on n'entend pas le son [ch] (de cheval).
PARTIAL/OCEAN/SUGAR/MASHED/FASHION/ MISSION/PRESSURE/ISSUE/RUSSIA/ DELICIOUS/SHEET/INVITATION/ RELATIONSHIP/DISH/CHEF/CHICKEN/ GINGER/OPTION/CHILLI/DECORATION

27. Circle the words whose pronunciation is correct.

a. curry ['k^{eu}ri]
b. era ['èri^{eu}]
c. beloved [bi'lovd]
d. variety [v^{eu}'raï^{eu}ti]
e. ale [èïl]

28. Trouvez les deux verbes mal accentués.
'INVENT/A'DAPT/'FOLLOW/'WHISTLE/ CON'SIST/'SWEETEN/'PUNISH/'CARRY/ DA'MAGE/'COMMENT/'SUFFER/CON'TAIN

....

UNIT 7

VOCABULARY INTERLUDE

29. Chassez l'intrus dans la liste suivante.
WHEAT/CORN/RICE/EGGPLANT/BARLEY/OATS/MILLET/RYE

30. Résolvez ces petites devinettes en trouvant les lettres manquantes.

a. I am a pseudo-cereal. Known as 'black wheat' in France, my use is widespread in Brittany. I am BU_ _ WHEAT.

b. We are a type of food high in carbohydrates, that includes rice, pasta, potatoes, and bread (called 'féculents' in French), we are S_ _ RCHY foods.

31. Match each French noun with its English translation.

- **a.** perdrix
- **b.** pintade
- **c.** dinde
- **d.** faisant
- **e.** oie
- **f.** caille

- **1.** pheasant
- **2.** goose
- **3.** turkey
- **4.** quail
- **5.** guinea fowl
- **6.** partridge

32. Entourez la ou les bonnes propositions.

a. The meat of chicken, duck, goose, or turkey is called:
1. giblets
2. venison
3. poultry

b. Pheasant, quail, partridge, and guinea fowl are (two possibilities):
1. giblets
2. game birds
3. fowl

c. The mixture of sausage meat, eggs, breadcrumbs, herbs, and spices, used to fill up poultry is the:
1. stuffing
2. breading
3. carving

d. The word 'gingerly' is a faux-ami, it means:
1. sans réfléchir
2. sans limite
3. avec précaution

e. « Se dégonfler » se dit :
1. to duck off
2. to chicken out
3. to goose on

33. Remettez les lettres dans l'ordre pour reconstituer ces noms de morceaux de poulet.

a. aile   GNIW   ....
b. pilon   MICSDUKRT   ....
c. cuisse   ELG   ....

34. Trouvez la traduction des épices en gras en résolvant ces énigmes.

a. **safran** : my first three letters are the same as in the expression '_ _ _ _ and sound'. My last four are the beginning of a word meaning 'the opposite of back'. _ _ _ _ _

b. **clous de girofle** : just change one letter in GLOVES ....

c. **fenouil en graines** : just change one letter in FENNEC ....

d. **muscade** : I'm composed of two words:

 + diminutive of 'Margaret'. ....

UNIT 7

35. Trouvez le légume de base de ces plats indiens d'accompagnement.

a. Dhal (very small dry bean):
_ _NTI_ _

b. Baignan Bartha (oval and purple vegetable):
E_ _ _PL_ _ _T

c. Aloo Gobi (type of white cabbage):
CA_ _ _IFLO_ _E_ _

d. Palak paneer (vegetable with dark green leaves):
PINA _ _

36. Complétez les espaces par *salt*, *curry* ou *rice*.

a. The twins are always together, like white on ....

b. Tom feels bad enough about failing his exam. Don't rub .... in the wound.

c. As usual, he will .... favour to the boss and get a promotion.

d. Don't believe everything he says. Take it with a pinch of ....

37. Les noms en gras sont dans la mauvaise phrase, remettez-les dans la bonne.

a. My car is neither green nor blue. It's neither fish nor **duck** → ....

b. He stopped smoking overnight, cold **chicken** → ....

c. Don't go in that bad neighbourhood alone. You'd be a sitting **goose** → ...., very vulnerable.

d. My father is no spring **fowl** → .... He's going to turn 70 next month.

e. Horror films scare me. They give me **turkey** → .... bumps every time.

38. Entourez la raison pour laquelle ces deux plats ont un nom qui prête à confusion.

a. chicken-fried steak
   1. contains no chicken
   2. is baked and not fried chicken

b. Bombay duck
   1. is not Indian but Irish
   2. is not duck meat but a type of fish dish

39. Associez chaque préparation culinaire indienne à sa description.

a. chutney ....
b. mango ....
c. lassi ....
d. samosa ....
e. Chai ....

   1. Fried snack or dish filled with various vegetables, herbs and/or meat.
   2. National fruit of India.
   3. Fruit or vegetable-based condiment.
   4. Indian tea, made with spices.
   5. Traditional yoghurt-based Indian drink.

40. Entourez la bonne proposition.

a. A(n) *Chinese/Indian/Greek* giver is someone who gives something and then claims it back.

b. *Chinese/Indian/Greek* whispers is a popular children's game ('téléphone arabe' in French).

c. If I don't understand a text at all, it's all *Chinese/Indian/Greek* to me.

d. 'Too many chiefs and not enough *Chinese/Indians/Greeks*' is a phrase used when too many people in a group want to be the boss, but not enough of them will actually do the job.

UNIT 7

BACK TO WORK – LAUGH AND LEARN

41. Correct the mistakes in these two texts.

a. Some people who are seek of the eternal Thansgiving turkey replace the traditionnal dish with an other

very original one: the turducken. Turducken is a stufed chicken, inside a stufed duck, inside a turkey!

The dish is said to have been invented by a cooker in Louisiana in the 1980s.

b. At a time when Victorians were falling in love with spicy Indian food, gentelmen were faced with a shoking

dilemma; indead doctors thought that spicy food made men horney and ressort to the terrible sin

of masturbation, so men were adviced to avoid spices and to eat bland food instead. That's how Graham's

crackers and Kellogg's corn flakes were invented in the USA at about the same time, as anti-masturbation

waypons, in an atempt to calm down mens' sexe drive!

42. Placez ces mots dans la bonne phrase pour reconstituer un proverbe.
ILLNESS/FLY/GRIEF/REAR

a. A(n) .... does not mind dying in coconut cream. (Swahili proverb)

b. It is better to be the head of a chicken than the .... of an ox. (Japanese proverb)

c. Just as medicine may not cure a serious ...., wine will certainly not dispel your .... (Chinese proverb)

43. Entourez le terme qui permet de reconstituer un proverbe.

a. Words are good, but fowls *lay/lie/lain* eggs. (German proverb)

b. When you cook a guinea fowl, the partridge gets *the/a/Ø* headache. (Nigerian proverb)

UNIT 7

44. Remettez les lettres des mots en majuscules dans l'ordre en vous aidant des indices fournis entre parenthèses, vous reconstituerez ainsi d'autres proverbes.

a. Laugh at the rice and you will PEWE' *(means 'cry')* .... for the lentil. (Southern US proverb)

b. Rice tastes good when RYPLOREP *(means 'well')* .... cooked, and talking is good when the opportunity is PERI *(means 'mature')* .... (Kashmir proverb)

c. The garlic complained to the onion, 'You KNITS *(slang for 'smell bad')* ....!" If you count your friend's SEKIMATS *(means 'errors')* .... , he will desert you. Many wars have been caused by a LISEGN *(means 'just one')* .... word.' (Arabian proverb)

45. Try and explain this joke.

'The plural of spouse is spice.' (Christopher Morley)

46. Placez les mots suivants dans la citation qui leur appartient.

TALK/ACCURATELY/TRUE/COUNT/CHICKEN/WAY

a. 'Chicken Tikka Masala is now a .... British national dish, not only because it is the most popular, but because it is a perfect illustration of the .... Britain absorbs and adapts external influences'. *(Robin Cook)*

b. 'My brother thinks he's a ....; we don't .... him out of it because we need the eggs.' *(Groucho Marx)*

c. 'People who .... their chickens before they are hatched act very wisely, because chickens run about so absurdly that it is impossible to count them ....' *(Oscar Wilde)*

47. Entourez la ou les expressions désignant le croupion de volaille.

    a. Parson's nose
    b. King's toe
    c. Pope's nose
    d. Queen's toe

UNIT 7

END-OF-CHAPTER TEST

48. Translate these sentences into English

1. Il est peu probable que les enfants n'aiment pas ton repas indien. Au contraire, ils adorent les blancs de volaille, en particulier de dinde ou de poulet. En plus, ils raffolent de ton smoothie au lait de noix de coco.

....

....

2. Il se peut que ton plat soit trop épicé si tu ajoutes du poivre. Tu ferais mieux de mettre moins de poivre et un peu plus d'ail.

....

....

3. Tu n'as pas besoin d'écraser le gingembre ; je l'ai déjà fait. Détends-toi et prends une bière blonde.

....

....

4. Comment ça, ça a le goût de safran ? Ce n'est pas possible. C'est bien marqué *paprika* sur le bocal !

....

....

5. Mon mari est très sensible aux épices fortes. Elles lui donnent mal à la tête. Plus les épices sont fortes et plus son mal de tête est intense. La cannelle ne lui fait pas de mal en revanche car elle est plutôt douce.

....

....

UNIT 8

Now let's go to the Emerald Isle and have some craic with a no-fuss, warming, and filling stew you will love sharing with family or friends on a cold autumn day. Dublin coddle is a dish of very humble origins, so the recipe relies on simple ingredients: pork sausages, bacon, potatoes, and onions.

Cooking coddle at the end of the week enabled the poorest households to use up the week's leftovers. The dish uses a slow-cooking method – the legend says that wives would leave the stew simmering and go to bed. Their husbands would find a nice and warm dinner when they got back from the pub. Irish people tend to eat coddle with soda bread – bread made with baking soda and buttermilk. Nowadays more than ever, the dish has all the pros: it's not going to hurt your wallet, everybody loves it, you don't have to be a chef at all to make it, and it is a dish you cannot spoil through lack of attention or overcooking since it can simmer on for hours with no adverse consequences. It is therefore perfect for overwhelmed families who don't have much time to attend the kitchen but still want to eat a nourishing meal. None of the cons then, you might wonder? Well, the dish will reveal all its Irishness when washed down with a good pint of Guinness, so you'd better check your local French store does sell the Black Nectar, or you might miss out on a nice Irish moment!

DUBLIN CODDLE

INGREDIENTS

4 SERVINGS:
- 1 kg of potatoes, peeled and thickly sliced
- 500 g of sausages, cut into large chunks
- 300 g of bacon or cooked ham, cut into thick strips
- 2 onions, peeled and thickly sliced
- 3 carrots, peeled and sliced
- 600 ml of chicken stock
- 3 tablespoons of chopped parsley
- salt and pepper

1. Cook the bacon and the sausages in a pan for five minutes. Place one layer of them in the bottom of an oven-proof casserole.

2. Layer alternately the remaining meat and the vegetables, seasoning each layer with parsley, salt, and pepper. Pour the chicken stock over the top.

3. Cover with a lid and cook at 180° C for about 2 hours. Take the lid off for at least 15 minutes, and add a few knobs of butter on top, so that it will crisp up and brown.

UNIT 8

QUESTIONS AROUND THE TEXT

1. Remettez les éléments dans l'ordre (rétablissez la ponctuation si nécessaire).

a. simple/city/coddle/Dublin/dish/a/very/of/is/with/the/associated

....

....

b. many/dish/drawbacks/almost/has/no/the/got/and/advantages

....

....

c. year/comfort/during/coddle/colder/is/the/of/appreciated/months/type/the/of/food/a

....

....

d. stout/pair/famous/customary/with/the/Irish/it/is/coddle/to

....

....

2. Trouvez les expressions imagées utilisées dans le texte pour désigner les éléments a. et b.

a. Ireland ....

b. a famous Irish beer ....

3. Find the missing letters of these words used in the texts.

a. Means 'fun' in Irish: __RAI__

b. Rassasiant : F__ __LIN__

c. When you peel potatoes, you R__MO__E their skin.

d. I overcooked the stew, and it burnt the __OT__OM of my saucepan.

e. Other word for 'shop': __ __ORE.

4. Trouvez et corrigez la lettre qui ne va pas dans les mots en gras (utilisés dans les textes).

a. When you ask yourself about something, you **wander** → ....

b. The **lip** → .... is what you cover the pot with.

c. You put your money and your I.D. in a **ballet** → ....

d. To **spare** → .... something is to divide it into equal portions.

e. Cooking coddle just below the boiling point is to **simper** → .... it.

5. Fill in the blanks in these rephrasings, using the words provided below.
GREATER/TROUBLE/MADE/TOO BUSY/ PAYING ENOUGH/TOO MUCH/CAN'T-FAIL/ANY UNFORTUNATE

a. 'Through lack of attention' (l. 15)
= by not .... attention

b. 'Overcooking' (l. 16) = cooking ....

c. 'overwhelmed' (l. 17) = being ....

d. 'it is a dish you cannot spoil' (l. 15)
= the dish is a ....

e. 'enabled the poorest households …' (l. 6-7)
= .... it possible for the poorest households

f. 'No-fuss' = (l. 1-2) ....-free

g. 'With no adverse consequences' (l. 16-17)
= without .... consequences

h. 'more than ever' (l. 12) = to a .... extent

UNIT 8

6. Fill in the blanks with *the* or *Ø*.

a. I heard on 1. .... radio that fewer and fewer people were reading 2. .... newspapers. I still buy my daily every morning. Yesterday there was an article comparing 3. .... Germany's economy with that of 4. .... Netherlands. I did not read it through, though. I could not concentrate because 5. .... neighbours were playing 6. .... guitar and their children were playing 7. .... tennis outside. There was an article about 8. .... pope too. I wanted to show you, but I forgot my newspaper on 9. .... train. Oh, I saw 10. .... Robinsons at 11. .... pub last night, by the way. They live in 12. .... village now, near 13. .... church.

b. I saw 1. .... Doctor O'Hara on 2. .... November 23rd. It was 3. .... last week. I usually see him on 4. .... Mondays but he had an emergency that day. We're almost in December already. 5. .... time does fly! Anyway, he is not 6. .... most tactful doctor out there. He said 7. .... heart was a wonderful organ but that 8. .... mine would not go much longer if I eat so much 9. .... fat. He told me to stop eating 10. .... recipes that use 11. .... cream or butter. Here's 12. .... list of 13. .... allowed recipes he gave me. Depressing. I don't like 14. .... winter vegetables!

7. Complétez ces expressions binaires, très courantes en anglais.
TAKE/SOUND/PROS/WEAR/LOUD/ENDS/QUIET/DO'S/
HUSTLE/GREY/SICK/SPAN

EXPRESSIONS	MEANING	EXPRESSIONS	MEANING
a. .... and cons	Avantages et inconvénients	**g.** .... and tired	Exaspéré, fatigué
b. give or	Plus ou moins, environ	**h.** .... and tear	Usure normale
c. .... and bustle	Agitation, tumulte, bousculade	**i.** spick and	Impeccable
d. peace and	Calme, quiétude	**j.** .... and dont's	Choses à faire et à ne pas faire
e. safe and	Sain et sauf	**k.** odds and	Bricoles, objets épars
f. .... and clear	Clair et net, bien clairement	**l.** old and	Dans ses vieux jours

UNIT 8

8. Formez un adjectif composé pertinent comme dans l'exemple fourni.

Ex. : a slow-cooking method = a method of cooking where the dish is cooked over a long period of time

a. a sweet	1. lasting	A. ....-................ soap has a nice fragrance.
b. a time	2. hand	B. ....-................ recipe allows you to save time.
c. a long	3. handed	C. ....-................ dish will go a long way.
d. right	4. smelling	D. ....-................ people do not handle things with their left hand.
e. a twelve	5. haired	E. ....-................ book contains more than ten recipes.
f. a second	6. saving	F. ....-................ table is not brand new.
g. long	7. recipe	G. ....-................ cooks are not allowed in kitchens as it is not hygienic.

9. Parmi les deux propositions, dites dans laquelle *still* a la même fonction que dans *but still want to eat a nourishing meal* (l. 18-19).

a. I know you are tired, still you could have called me.

b. I still live in London.

10. Complétez les espaces par *in*, *for*, *on*, *from* ou *Ø*.

a. He entered .... the room singing.

b. I borrowed this recipe .... a friend.

c. How do you account .... the smoked taste?

d. I can't resist .... bacon.

e. The taste depends .... the amount of bacon used.

f. Paul survived .... the plane crash.

g. How much did you pay .... that phone?

h. Did you participate .... the cooking?

i. The new menu was imposed .... the cooks.

j. Her creativity has resulted .... amazing new recipes.

11. Circle the right preposition.

a. My coddle was not so good. I'm *off/out/on* of practice!

b. I don't know this recipe at all. I'll have to read it *on/to/in* detail.

c. My husband does not like people who are always late. Please come at seven *on/off/to* the dot.

d. 'The meat was cooked *off/on/to* a turn' means that it was cooked *into/on/to* perfection.

e. His cooking improvisation was *out/off/on* the mark. The flavours did not match.

UNIT 8

12. Correct the mistakes in these sentences (if any).

a. The farmer grows potatoes. ....

b. Coddle keeps itself well for a few days. ....

c. The potatoes have the same size. ....

d. They asked me to come. ....

e. They should discuss of the recipes. ....

f. Wait me, please. ....

g. He explained to me how to make coddle. ....

h. Does she trust him? ....

i. He told to me he was a vegan. ....

j. Have you said to them you were Irish? ....

13. Dites quelle préposition manque dans les phrases suivantes (une seule par bloc).

a. I'm .... the verge of fainting. I'll have a snack .... the go, just to be .... the safe side.

Préposition : ....

b. .... addition to buying vegetables .... bulk, you should also buy more meat.

.... a nutshell, you don't buy enough ingredients to run the restaurant .... the long run.

Préposition : ....

c. I was .... a loss for words .... first. My job was .... stake, and I wanted to keep unemployment .... bay, but you can't work two jobs .... the same time for long.

Préposition : ....

14. Résolvez les devinettes suivantes (les mots à deviner se cachent dans la liste fournie ci-dessous).

ATTENTION/ATTEND/CHUNK/ISLE/WALLET/WOULD/OVERWHELMED/AUTUMN/DUBLIN/TEND/EMERALD/HALF/NOWADAYS/PROS/SPOIL/ADVERSE/CHEF/HUSBANDS/CONS/HOUSEHOLDS/BUTTERMILK/CHECK/CHOPPED

a. Mon *s* ne se prononce pas, je suis le mot ....

b. Mon *n* ne se prononce pas, je suis le mot ....

c. Notre *l* ne se prononce pas, nous sommes les mots ....

d. Mon *ch* ne se prononce pas [tch], je suis le mot ....

UNIT 8

15. Find and circle the statement that is wrong.

a. *Isle* (l. 1) se prononce comme *aisle* (['aïl]).

b. *Says* (l. 8) se prononce comme *16* en français.

c. *Parsley* (recette, 2.) rime avec *grey*.

16. Parmi ces mots de trois ou quatre syllabes, entourez ceux qui vous semblent bien accentués.

'EMERALD/FA'MILY/IN'GREDIENTS/PO'TATOES,/'SAUSAGES/PO'SSIBLE/
'NOURISHING/'BANANA/YES'TERDAY/'NOVEMBER/CA'THEDRAL/'DIFFICULT/
DIS'HONEST/'ELEVEN/VA'NILLA/'CELERY/A'MERICAN/'CONSEQUENCES/OVER'WHELMED/
VEGE'TABLES

17. En vous aidant de cette liste de mots correctement accentués, complétez la règle.

'household – 'leftovers – 'soda bread – 'buttermilk – 'tablespoons

Règle d'accentuation:

Les noms .... sont accentués sur le .... mot.

VOCABULARY INTERLUDE

18. À l'aide des lettres fournies dans les bulles ci-dessous, formez la traduction des mots suivants.

a. .... ham (jambon blanc)

b. .... ham (jambon cru)

c. .... ham (jambon fumé)

d. .... (côtelette de porc)

e. .... (lardons)

19. Entourez dans la liste suivante la seule pièce de viande de porc (tranche épaisse de jambon salé ou fumé).

a. chuck

b. gizzard

c. drumstick

d. gammon

e. plate

UNIT 8

20. Reliez chaque type de préparation des pommes de terre à son équivalent français.

- **a.** mashed
- **b.** crisps
- **c.** scalloped
- **d.** hash browns, rosti
- **e.** fries, chips
- **f.** boiled
- **g.** baked
- **h.** fried

- **1.** en galettes, cuites en poêle à frire
- **2.** à l'eau
- **3.** sautées
- **4.** au gratin
- **5.** en purée
- **6.** en chips
- **7.** en frites
- **8.** en robe des champs

21. À partir des phrases suivantes, devinez ce que signifient les expressions en gras.

1. s'empiffrer
2. avoir deux mains gauches
3. en faire des tonnes
4. un pansement sur une jambe de bois
5. sauver la mise de quelqu'un

a. You can polish your old car but it'll be **lipstick on a pig**. (….)

b. Thank you for **saving my bacon** during the meeting. I really needed some help. (….)

c. Don't **pork out on** the coddle. Save some room for dessert. (….)

d. She **hams it up** in front of people, but she's not sincere. (….)

e. Don't ask me to help you fix your sink. I am **ham-fisted**. (….)

22. Entourez la bonne proposition.

a. I'll do it very quickly. I'll do it in *a pig's whisper/ a pig's eye*.

b. He does nothing but watch tv and eat crisps. He's a *small potato/couch potato*.

c. They are very good people, the *salt of the earth/ bacon of the earth*.

d. No one wants to deal with this question. It's a *ham/pig's tail/hot potato*.

e. I can't afford to lose my job. I bring home the *potatoes/bacon/salt*.

f. John is really not reliable. He's not worth his *bacon/potatoes/salt*.

23. Circle the correct proposition.

1. En Angleterre, les petites saucisses enrobées de bacon (traditionnellement consommées en hors-d'œuvre) s'appellent :

a. Angels on horseback
b. Pigs in blankets
c. Devils on horseback

2. Un sausage roll est :

a. un friand à la saucisse
b. un hot dog (sous sa dénomination anglaise)
c. un petit rouleau à pâtisserie

87

UNIT 8

BACK TO WORK – LAUGH AND LEARN

24. Lisez le texte suivant, puis dites si les affirmations qui suivent sont vraies ou fausses.

In Irish people's lives, the word *craic* – pronounced 'crack' – is a bit like the word *smurf* in the land of the little blue men, where it is used over and over in different contexts, with varying meanings. Yes, we said previously that it means something like 'fun', but we were oversimplifying things for practical reasons.

The problem is no one can really define the word, and it cannot be translated into English. If an Irishman asks you, 'How's the craic?' or 'What's the craic?' he is just greeting you, asking 'How are you? What's new?' Now if he suggests to 'go have some craic', it can mean many things. *Having craic* means something like 'having a good time, having fun'. For example, if someone is a great craic, you have fun with them. If people really enjoyed a party, they will say, 'We had great craic'. And if the craic was really good, they will say that the craic was 'ninety' (or 'mighty'). However, craic is a social thing – if you are watching a film alone at home, that's not craic, even if you're having a really good time. Finally, craic has much to do with the atmosphere itself, and these things in particular participate in building up craic: people you really like, a lot of talking and joking, good music, and a few drinks.

	VRAI	FAUX
a. *Craic* se prononce comme 'crush'.	☐	☐
b. *Mighty craic* est un juron.	☐	☐
c. Si l'on dit de quelqu'un qu'il est *a great craic*, cela signifie que cette personne est séduisante.	☐	☐
d. *Craic* est un concept plutôt qu'un simple mot.	☐	☐
e. *How's the craic?* est une formule détendue similaire à *what's up?*	☐	☐
f. Le *craic* se partage forcément autour d'un bon repas.	☐	☐

25. Chassez l'intrus (bière américaine parmi des bières irlandaises).

a. Guinness
b. Harp Lager
c. O'Hara's
d. Budweiser
e. Murphy's
f. Kilkenny
g. Porterhouse

UNIT 8

26. Trouvez les mots cachés dans cette grille en vous aidant des indices fournis (mots utilisés dans le texte de l'exercice 24).

a. *schtroumpf* en anglais
b. guy from Ireland
c. synonyme de *before*
d. simplify too much
e. saluer
f. super craic
g. telling funny stories

W	W	H	I	R	I	S	H	M	A	N	D	X	K
G	V	T	Q	U	M	Y	R	X	P	O	V	C	D
S	R	H	M	U	B	N	S	C	D	A	G	K	L
K	M	O	V	E	R	S	I	M	P	L	I	F	Y
I	L	U	J	O	K	I	N	G	Q	W	R	X	J
U	Z	P	R	P	B	U	T	C	R	W	J	U	Q
B	M	H	S	F	Z	B	M	R	T	E	A	O	K
Z	D	H	O	R	T	S	W	H	X	P	E	S	R
O	Z	X	F	T	O	R	V	G	B	L	R	T	Z
S	C	Q	F	M	M	G	R	M	V	P	D	M	C
D	M	I	G	H	T	Y	Q	Q	W	I	J	D	O
Q	U	J	W	T	C	R	A	I	G	Y	K	P	D
Q	V	L	G	G	B	G	S	A	I	P	M	W	D
Y	N	P	R	E	V	I	O	U	S	L	Y	M	I

27. Lisez le texte ci-dessous, puis remettez chaque mot en gras dans la phrase qui devrait normalement lui être attribuée.

A few years ago, researchers from Guinness made some calculations and found out that more than 150,000 pints of Ireland's most famous stout disappeared in men's beards and moustaches every year. Speaking of alcohol, the Irish vocabulary for describing the state of being drunk is rich: they will say they are *twisted and sozzled, locked, plastered, paralytic, langered, ossified, suttered,* or *fluthered,* among other possibilities! The Irish have an interesting vocabulary generally speaking. They are not very tired but *banjaxed*, they'll ask you to stop *olagonin'* if you're complaining on and on about something, they will say you are *blaggarding* if you annoy them, or *acting the maggot* if you're being a fool. And they'll have none of your *shenanigans* (manigances)!

a. Fifteen thousand pints of Guinness are **behaviours** → .... in men's facial hair in Ireland each year.
b. In Irish slang, *banjaxed* means **plastered** → ....
c. The Irish have many words to describe drunkenness, such as **exhausted** → ....
d. You are *blaggarding* Irish people if you are making them **wasted** → ....
e. They think there's something worm-like about silly **angry** → ....!

28. Entourez les trois plats traditionnels irlandais à base de pomme de terre.

a. Colcannon
b. Crubeens
c. Boxty
d. Champ
e. Barmbrack

29. Entourez le nom de pub dublinois qui existe vraiment.

a. The Flirting Lemon
b. The Smelly Lemon
c. The Hairy Lemon

UNIT 8

30. En prenant la première lettre des devinettes suivantes, vous trouverez les mots mystères…

a. 'The Irish ignore anything they can't .... (1) or .... (2).' (James Boswell, Scottish writer)

b. 'God invented .... (3) to keep the Irish from ruling the world.' (Ed McMahon)

c. 'Because that's still how Irish people are seen, as *twinkly-eyed* fuckers with a pig under their arm, high-stepping it around the world, going, "I'll paint your house now, but watch out, I might steal the .... (4) later, ohohoho!" Which is only half true!' (Dylan Moran)

(1)	(2)	(3)	(4)
capital city of Ireland ▪ _ _ _ _ _ _	patron saint of Ireland ▪ _ _ _ _ _ _ _	seven days ▪ _ _ _	capital city of England ▪ _ _ _ _ _ _
not imaginary ▪ _ _ _ _	your father's brother ▪ _ _ _ _	sixty minutes ▪ _ _ _ _	opposite of dead ▪ _ _ _ _ _
country of pasta ▪ _ _ _ _ _	11th month of the year ▪ _ _ _ _ _ _ _ _	sick ▪ _ _	evening meal ▪ _ _ _ _ _
opposite of South ▪ _ _ _ _	not hot ▪ _ _ _ _	not quick ▪ _ _ _ _	American currency ▪ _ _ _ _ _
room where you cook ▪ _ _ _ _ _ _ _	50 % ▪ _ _ _	fruit and bird from New-Zealand ▪ _ _ _ _	opposite of full ▪ _ _ _ _ _
		opposite of difficult ▪ _ _ _ _	water from the sky ▪ _ _ _ _
		'miam' in English ▪ _ _ _ _ _	

UNIT 8

END-OF-CHAPTER TEST

31. Translate these sentences into English

1. Je me demande si vous pourrez résister à ce ragoût à cuisson lente. Il est très rassasiant et se conserve bien pendant plusieurs jours.

....

....

2. J'aurais aimé partager ce repas avec vous. Malheureusement je suis débordé cette semaine. Ne m'attendez pas pour manger.

....

....

3. J'en ai plus qu'assez que le chef fasse brûler tous les fonds de casseroles. Regarde, les oignons sont encore trop cuits. Je ne lui fais pas confiance. De plus, la cuisine n'est pas propre. Elle devrait toujours être impeccable. La réputation du restaurant est en jeu !

....

....

4. Il m'a expliqué qu'il ne fallait pas enlever le couvercle tout de suite, mais attendre une heure au moins. C'est le seul inconvénient de cette recette.

....

....

UNIT 9

Chutney is a condiment made with chopped vegetables, fresh and/or dried fruit, various spices and herbs, sugar, and vinegar. It comes from India, where the tradition is to serve nearly every meal with little bowls of chutney on the side. The British discovered the delights of chutney during the colonial era and adopted it, giving it a little British twist. Today, to many British people, chutney means Major Grey's mango chutney, but the combinations of ingredients used in a chutney are so endless that the only limit is that of your imagination. It therefore comes in countless shapes, colours, tastes, and textures. The flavours can go from more or less spicy, to sweet and fruity, sour, minty, tangy, or citrusy, and the texture can vary from that of a smooth jam to that of a chunky fruit salad. Chutney is traditionally served with curried foods, but it is a very versatile condiment that can equally enhance flavours and soften dishes that are on the spicy side. It will also kick everything up a notch: from cheese, curries, sandwiches, and crackers to meats. It works wonders as a dip as well. It is no coincidence that the condiment is a must in a traditional British picnic-like dish called the *ploughman's lunch*, still popular in most pubs. The dish is composed of cheese, thick slices of bread, thick ham, butter, pickle, and a dollop of chutney, served with a pint of beer or cider.

APPLE & PLUM CHUTNEY

INGREDIENTS

ONE JAR:
- 4 cooking apples (such as Granny Smith), peeled, cored, and diced
- 1.5 kg of purple plums, pitted and diced
- 2 large red onions, chopped
- 2 teaspoons of grated fresh ginger
- 1 teaspoon of cinnamon powder
- 1/2 teaspoon of clove powder
- 3 garlic cloves, crushed
- 1 tablespoon of salt
- 1/2 teaspoon of pepper
- 450 ml of wine or cider vinegar
- 400 g of brown sugar

1. Put all the ingredients in a pot or pan and mix well so that the fruit pieces are well coated with spices, sugar, and vinegar.

2. Bring to a boil, stirring regularly, and leave to simmer without a lid on for about one hour (until you get a thick texture).

3. In the meantime, sterilise a jar (the easiest way is to boil it for a few minutes).

4. Pour the mixture into the sterilised jar and seal well. You can eat it immediately after cooling, but chutney develops all its flavours over a little time's maturation. So try and be patient for a few weeks. It's worth the wait!

UNIT 9

QUESTIONS AROUND THE TEXT

1. Séparez les mots au bon endroit en rétablissant la ponctuation, puis dites si les affirmations sont vraies ou fausses.

VRAI **FAUX**

a. chutneyisaverygenerictermfortwotypesofcondimentsspicyorsourones.

b. itiscustomarytoservealittlechutneywithmealsinIndia.

c. chutneyiscommonlyservedalongsideaclassicpubdishcalledploughman'slunch.

d. chutneyisafastidiouscondimentasitcanonlybeusedwithfewspecificfoodslikemeats.

2. Remettez les lettres dans l'ordre pour retrouver les saveurs évoquées dans le texte.

a. épicé   PYSIC   ....
b. sucré   EWEST   ....
c. fruité   RIFTUY   ....
d. aigre   ROSU   ....
e. mentholé YTIMN   ....
f. acidulé   GATNY   ....
g. d'agrumes SICYTRU   ....

3. Complétez cette grille de mots avec le vocabulaire du texte et de la recette.

Across

2. noyau
4. régal, plaisir
7. bonne dose, bonne cuillerée
8. verser
9. fermer hermétiquement
10. porc cuit et servi en tranches

Down

1. vin
3. condiments au vinaigre
5. trognon de pomme
6. pot à confiture
8. prune

UNIT 9

4. Résolvez ces petites énigmes.

a. We are two adjectives from the text, and we both mean 'infinite.' Who are we? ..../....................

b. I am an English proverb that means 'the only limit is that of your imagination' (l. 9). Who am I?

    1. The sea is the limit.   **2.** The sun is the limit.   **3.** The sky is the limit.

c. The recipe talks about us. We are the opposite of 'eating apples' (pommes à croquer). Who are we? ....

5. Trouvez les lettres manquantes de ces mots utilisés dans le texte ou la recette.

a. faux ami, signifie *polyvalent* __ER__ATI__E

b. relever une saveur (ici) E__ __ AN__E

c. adoucir S__F__E__

d. sauce pour tremper __I__

e. signifie *laboureur* __LOU__ __ __ AN

f. signifie *refroidir* __ O __ L

g. signifie *lisse, doux* S__OO__ __

6. Complétez les reformulations suivantes en plaçant les éléments fournis ci-dessous dans la bonne phrase.

EFFICIENT/ALMOST/FOR/FROM/WHY/HARDLY/AS A RESULT/BETTER

a. 'it therefore comes in countless shapes' (l. 9-10) = ... , it comes in countless shapes

b. 'nearly every meal with... chutney' (l. 3-4) = ... no meal is without chutney

c. almost never without chutney = ... ever without chutney

d. 'It's worth the wait' (recette, 4.) = It is worth waiting ....

e. 'to many British people' (l. 6-7) = ... the British point of view

f. 'it works wonders' (l. 17) = it is very .... with

g. 'it is no coincidence' (l. 18) = it is the very reason ....

h. 'kick everything up a notch' (l. 16) = make everything much ....

7. Find the conjunction that is missing in the blank spaces (one and the same).

.... I told you, there is no such thing .... too much spice! .... an Indian person, I love chilli, ... my father did.

UNIT 9

8. Fill in the blanks with either *and* **or** *or*.

a. A question of life .... death.
b. I use one kilo of sugar, give .... take.
c. I should have used more ginger. Oh well, live .... learn.
d. Rain .... shine, my aunt would make chutney every year.
e. Try .... buy sweeter plums next time.
f. I almost overcooked my chutney. It was touch .... go.
g. Don't add more sugar right now. Wait .... see how the cooking goes.
h. I can't read the recipe without my glasses on. Go .... get them for me.

9. Trouvez le seul et même adverbe/ adjectif qui manque dans le texte suivant.

Until the condiments arrived, it was 'so .... so good,' but then the chutney was .... too mild, a .... cry from the one you eat in India, and the jar was .... too small for twelve guests. On the whole, this Indian party was .... from being a success.

10. Complétez les espaces par *a(n)*, *the* **ou** *Ø*.

a. That was such .... good chutney you offered us for .... lunch!
b. It can be hard to live without .... car and .... internet.
c. My teenage boys have .... appetite. I need to cook huge portions.
d. What .... pity you're in .... hurry and can't stay for .... dinner.
e. .... mangoes were ten pounds .... kilo .... last week at .... market.

11. Correct the mistakes in the use of articles when necessary.

a. Queen Elizabeth is said to have the sense of humour.
....
b. The neighbours are making a noise again.
....
c. Their son has become entrepreneur and has made a fortune. What wonderful surprise!
....
....
d. The rich have tendency to think that they have a right to better food.
....
....

12. Fill in the blanks with *right, well* **or** *good*.

a. Erin has always been a .... cook, she can cook chutney very ....
b. The ploughman's platter was .... presented.
c. Keith, you're the .... man at the .... time. I need your opinion on my chutney.
d. My jam is generally .... but I can't cook .... chutney, though.
e. ...., I think you're .... My chutney could do with more sugar.

UNIT 9

13. Remettez ces traductions dans l'ordre.

a. Je vais généralement travailler en voiture le lundi.
→ on/drive/work/Mondays/usually/to/I
....

b. Mon patron a travaillé à s'en rendre malade.
→ sick/himself/boss/worked/my/has
....

c. Le chien de la voisine s'est enfui (en courant).
→ away/dog/neighbour's/the/ran
....

d. J'ai astiqué la marmite à chutney jusqu'à ce qu'elle soit propre.
→ clean/chutney/have/pot/scrubbed/the/I
....

e. Tu m'as persuadé de faire du chutney.
→ making/into/you/have/me/chutney/talked
....

f. Il a usé de menaces pour me faire démissionner.
→ into/he/quitting/me/threatened
....

14. Pour chacun de ces verbes, entourez la bonne particule.

a. She broke *down/into/up* with her boyfriend.
The burglar broke *down/into/up* the house.
My car broke *down/into/up* this morning.

b. I will come *back/off/on* to this Indian restaurant.
I will call *back/off/on* you tonight if you're home.
The concert was called *back/off/on* because of the rain.

c. I have diabetes. I need to keep *on/off/up* chutney.
You're reading the recipe too fast. I can't keep *on/off/up* with you.
Keep *on/off/up* stirring the chutney. Don't stop.

d. I look like my mother, but I also take *out/to/after* my dad.
Could you take *out/to/after* the bin?
My husband took *out/to/after* cooking a few years ago.

15. Fill in the blanks with these particles.
OUT/TO/OUT/INTO/UP/OFF/ACROSS

a. I bumped .... Ian at the post office.
b. I came .... this recipe book at the library.
c. I only found .... yesterday that he was married.
d. I'm looking forward .... meeting you soon.
e. Could you pick me .... at the airport?
f. He pointed .... that the chutney was rather bitter.
g. The meeting was put .... until next week.

16. Reformulez en remplaçant les noms soulignés par le pronom personnel correspondant.

a. Give up <u>smoking</u> = ...
b. Take <u>your shoes</u> off = ...

UNIT 9

17. Reliez chaque début de nom à particule à la suite qui lui correspond.

- **a.** an out...
- **b.** a let ...
- **c.** an ...look
- **d.** a set ...
- **e.** a mix ...

- **1.** down (a disappointment)
- **2.** up (a confusion)
- **3.** out... (a way you see things)
- **4.** come (a result)
- **5.** back (a problem)

18. Entourez la ou les lettres silencieuses dans les mots suivants.

a. ploughman   **b.** soften   **c.** plum

19. Tell if these statements are right or wong.   RIGHT   WRONG

a. *pour* (recette, 4.) se prononce comme *power*.

b. *Cored* (cf. début liste ingrédients) rime avec *pitted* (cf. début liste ingrédients).

c. Les suffixes *-ful*, *-able*, *-ing*, *-ed*, *-dom*, *-ly* et *-ness* ne déplacent pas l'accent, par conséquent on aura : 'wonder → 'wonderful; 'read → read'able; eat → eat'ing; taste → 'tasted; free → free'dom; 'light → 'lightly; 'happy → 'happiness.

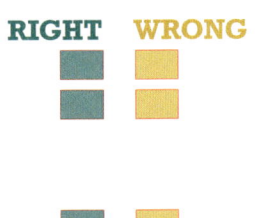

20. Entourez les mots dans lesquels on entend le son *[ou]*.
FRUIT/SUGAR/SOUR/SMOOTH/FLAVOURS/PLUM/COOLING/POUR/BLOOD/FLEW

21. Trouvez les mots utilisés dans le texte ou la recette, auxquels font référence ces devinettes.

a. Mon homophone signifie *phoque* ....

b. Mon homophone signifie *pauvre* ....

c. Mon homophone est un adjectif qui signifie *accord* (musique) ....

d. Mon homophone signifie *poids* ....

22. Entourez la bonne prononciation.

a. versatile (l. 14)
  1. ['veuss^{eu}til]
  2. ['veuss^{eu}taïl]
  3. ['veussatil]

b. citrus (l. 12)
  1. ['sitruss]
  2. ['saïtrus]
  3. ['saïtr^{eu}ss]

UNIT 9

VOCABULARY INTERLUDE

23. En prenant la première lettre des mots à trouver, vous obtiendrez le nom de la famille à laquelle appartiennent les fruits suivants.
LEMON/LIME/GRAPEFRUIT/BLOOD ORANGE/TANGERINE

a. blue, green, or yellow: ▢ _ _ _ _ _
b. country of St Patrick: ▢ _ _ _ _ _
c. favourite English drink: ▢ _ _
d. opposite of wrong: ▢ _ _ _ _
e. really bad looking: ▢ _ _ _
f. summer or winter: ▢ _ _ _ _ _

24. Trouvez le nom d'agrume manquant dans les phrases suivantes (le même).
a. He is very disappointed. The car he bought is a ....
b. You're so annoying Andy, go suck a ....!

25. Trouvez la traduction anglaise des fruits suivants dans la grille.
a. raisin sec
b. figue
c. datte
d. papaye
e. ananas
f. mangue
g. pruneau
h. coing

```
P R U N E O K N U Z
B H J Z H Y I O J Y
R Z Z M U S C E D W
K F Q U I N C E V R
I Z I A P A P A Y A
X T R G R C S T B Q
N X M A N G O C B U
J N L B D A T E P X
S P I N E A P P L E
X H F V B U N Z Q X
```

26. Les mots en gras sont placés dans la mauvaise phrase. Remettez-les dans la bonne.
a. 'When life gives you **a(n) fig** → .... , make lemonade' means make the most of bad circumstances.
b. I don't care **a(n) apple** → .... about football. I could not care less!
c. '**Bananas** → .... a day keeps the doctor away' is an English proverb.
d. He's going to go **lemons** → .... when he hears you bumped his car!

UNIT 9

27. Circle the right proposition.

a. If someone speaks with *a plum/a mango/a lemon* in their mouth, they speak with an accent that is typical of a high social class.

b. My sister is very different from me. We are like *apples and oranges/lemons and oranges/apples and plums*.

c. You should experience things! Variety is the *tang/spice/mint* of life.

d. I hate those political parties who never act. They're all talk and no *beer/ham/cider*.

28. Fill in the blanks with either *cheese*, *bread* or *apple*.

a. He loves her very much. She's the .... of his eye.

b. Mr. Eliot doesn't want to spend any money. He's a ....-sparing old man.

c. The internet has been the best thing since sliced ....

d. Ian is just like his parents. The .... does not fall far from the tree.

BACK TO WORK – LAUGH AND LEARN

29. Correct the mistakes in this text.

Chutney is not only a condiment, it is as well a type of music from the south Caribbean, that has a fast bit.

It was borne in Trinidad & Tobago, created by Indo-Caribbeans – the descendents of 19th century West Indies

immigrants. The music has its routs in Indian folk music, and has incorporated calypso and soca. Chutney

use to be sang allmost exclusively by fimale musicians and singers, and the songs' lirics were manely religious.

The most famous chutney singer is Sundar Popo, a.k.a. 'The King of Chutney,' who became popular in 1970

with a hit song called *Nana & Nani*. More ricently chutney music has been enriched by other genres like

dancehall music and reggae.

Just know that in slang, chutney is also used to refer at various human body fluids, but we will not go there, yuck.

UNIT 9

30. Placez ces termes dans la bonne citation.

AMAZING/PROVIDED/THIRST/UNLESS

a. 'My mother used to say, "The older you get, the better you get, ... you're a banana".' (The Golden Girls)

b. 'Honey bees are .... creatures. I mean, think about it, do earwigs make chutney?' (Eddie Izzard)

c. 'Americans can eat garbage, ... you sprinkle it liberally with ketchup, mustard, chilli sauce, tabasco sauce, cayenne pepper, or any other condiment which destroys the original flavor of the dish.' (Henry Miller)

d. 'To offer friendship to one who is looking for love is like giving bread to someone dying of ....' (Spanish proverb)

31. À une ou deux lettre(s) près, les mots en gras sont incorrects. Apportez la correction nécessaire.

a. 'Never buy bread **FROG** → .... a butcher.' (Irish proverb)

b. 'Don't bite till you know **WEATHER** → .... it is bread or a stone.' (Italian proverb)

c. 'Everybody's got to **RELIEVE** → .... in something. I **RELIEVE** → .... I'll have another beer.' (W.C. Fields)

d. 'Cheese is **COLD** → .... in the morning, silver at noon, and lead at night.' (German proverb)

END-OF-CHAPTER TEST

32. Translate these sentences into English

1. J'ai hâte de goûter à ton chutney à la mangue et aux agrumes. Je suis certain que son côté acidulé fait des merveilles avec de la volaille. Va en chercher.

....
....
....

2. Cela vaut le coup de garder ces pots en verre car ils sont très polyvalents. Personnellement je m'en sers pour y stocker mon chutney.

....
....
....

3. Comme il l'a souligné, cette recette est inratable, à condition d'utiliser des pommes à cuire et d'éviter les pommes à croquer.

....
....
....

4. Pourrais-tu verser le chutney dans les pots et les sceller ? Cette fournée est un peu trop lisse à mon goût, tant pis. La prochaine fois, essaie de mettre des fruits secs.

....
....
....

5. Tu m'as persuadé d'utiliser plus de chutney dans ma cuisine au quotidien. C'est vrai que ses possibilités d'utilisation sont infinies. Le délice d'un bon chutney sur du pain croustillant par exemple est souvent sous-estimé.

....
....
....
....

UNIT 10

Everybody likes cake, right? So, for our first dessert recipe, let's go to the Land Down Under and learn how to bake its national cake, the Lamington, shall we? Although there is a bone of contention over its origin with New Zealand, who claims it invented it first, it has generally been presented as an Australian cake, named after Baron Lamington, who was Governor of the State of Queensland from 1895 to 1901. Lamington cake is a square-shaped sponge cake, iced with melted chocolate, and coated in desiccated coconut. Most of the cake's appeal lies in the delicate balance of flavours and textures between the moistness of the sponge cake, the sweetness of the chocolate, and the crunchiness of the coconut. In some variations, the sponge cake is filled with tangy fruit jam so as to counterbalance the sweetness of the chocolate and add extra texture. This little addition will tempt those with a sweet tooth, but it can also disturb that balance. As far as presentation is concerned, the whole cake is generally cut into small individual-serving squares. Since coffee compliments chocolate well, a cup of joe is one of the best companions to Lamington there is. However, we advise you not to pair it with just any kind of coffee, but to indulge yourself in a nice Irish coffee.

LAMINGTON CAKE

INGREDIENTS

BATCH OF 12:

For the cake:
- 200 g of flour
- 2 teaspoons of baking powder
- 1 pinch of salt
- 60 g of butter, at room temperature
- 60 g of sugar
- 60 ml of milk
- 1/2 teaspoon of vanilla extract
- 1 egg, at room temperature

For the icing:
- 225 g of icing sugar
- 50 g of cocoa powder
- 1 tablespoon of butter, melted
- 60 ml of warm milk
- 225 g of grated coconut

For the Irish coffee (1 cup):
- 60 ml of cold whipping cream
- 2 tablespoons of brown sugar
- 40 ml of whiskey
- 175 ml of hot and strong fresh coffee

You can make the sponge cake yourself (steps 1 to 4) or use a ready-to-bake sponge cake if you are in a rush.

1. Preheat the oven to 200° C. Grease and flour your baking dish.

2. Make the cake. Beat the butter and the sugar in a large bowl. Add the egg, stir, and add the vanilla.

3. Add the flour, the baking powder, and the salt. Pour in the milk, mixing until you get a smooth batter.

4. Pour the batter into the dish and bake for 20 minutes. Leave to cool.

5. Prepare the icing: combine the icing sugar and the cocoa in a large bowl. Add the warm milk and the melted butter, and mix until you get a thick but fluid icing.

6. When the cake has cooled, cut it into 12 squares. Pour the icing and the coconut into two separate bowls. Dip each square in the chocolate icing before rolling it in the coconut.

7. Make the Irish coffee: pour the whiskey into a cup. Add the sugar and stir until it is dissolved. Add the coffee and stir. Whip the cream lightly and put one tablespoon on top.

UNIT 10

QUESTIONS AROUND THE TEXT

1. Remettez les groupes de mots dans l'ordre pour former quelques énoncés factuels sur le *Lamington cake* évoqués dans le texte.

a. the origin/between Aussies/there is/and Kiwis over/of Lamington cake/a disagreement
....

b. shredded coconut/layers sponge/Lamington cake/chocolate, and/cake, melted
....

c. is that/of a/good thing/be too much/adding jam/the con of/it may
....

d. higher level/bring the tasting/Irish coffee will/to a/of Lamington cake
....

2. Classify these items in the following table.
KIWIS/LAND OF THE LONG WHITE CLOUD/AUSSIES/LAND DOWN UNDER

	COUNTRY'S NICKNAME	INHABITANTS' NICKNAME
AUSTRALIA		
NEW ZEALAND		

3. Circle the correct proposition(s).

a. Someone coming from New Zealand is a:
  1. New Zealander
  2. New Zealandor
  3. New Zealandman

b. The jam in Lamington is:
  1. compulsory
  2. optional
  3. ludicrous

c. According to Kiwis, Lamington cake is:
  1. an Australian invention
  2. a New Zealander invention

d. Lord Lamington was Governor of Queensland:
  1. at the turn of the nineteenth century
  2. in the late nineteenth century
  3. towards the end of the nineteenth century

e. 'to advise' (l. 20) means:
  1. to recommand
  2. to recommend
  3. to recomend

UNIT 10

4. Trouvez dans cette grille les mots anglais, utilisés dans le texte, auxquels font allusion les indices.

a. Slang for *coffee* : ....
b. Se faire plaisir : to .... yourself
c. Une pomme de discorde : a .... of contention
d. Prétendre (faux ami) : to ....
e. Le moelleux : ....
f. Le croquant : ....
g. Acidulé : ....
h. Perturber, déranger : ....

5. Complete the following rephrasings.

a. 'those with a sweet tooth' (l. 15)
→ those w____ ____ve a sweet tooth.
b. 'will appeal to those with a sweet tooth'
= those who like __uga__ will enj____ it.

6. Attribuez le bon suffixe nominal aux termes suivants (*ness*, *dom*, *ship* ou *hood*).

a. bitter...................
b. sour...................
c. bore...................
d. star...................
e. wis...................
f. owner...................
g. man...................
h. empti...................
i. child...................
j. sick...................
k. sad...................
l. forgive...................

7. Rephrase the following sentences, as shown in the example.

Ex.: <u>He failed</u> the exam. It surprised me.
→ <u>His failure</u> surprised me.

a. <u>They refused</u> to help me.
→ .... surprised me.
b. <u>She explained</u> the lesson.
→ .... was very clear.
c. <u>We accept</u> that life is hard sometimes.
→ .... is necessary.
d. <u>You arrived</u> just in time.
→ .... was in the nick of time.

UNIT 10

8. Rephrase the following sentences, as shown in the example.

Ex.: Your answer was urgent.
→ I emphasised the urgency of it.

a. We have been intimate for months.
→ Our .... began months ago.

b. Your decision was certain.
→ I expected the .... of your decision.

c. Liam is fluent at English.
→ His English .... is impressive.

d. They said the info was secret.
→ The .... of the info is important.

e. Your explanation was clear.
→ I appreciate the .... of your explanation.

9. Trouvez l'adjectif dérivé des mots soulignés.

a. I don't want to disturb you.
→ Your arrival was .... to me.

b. He makes decisions easily.
→ He is very ....

c. The gesture signifies much.
→ The gesture was ....

d. Sugar appeals to children.
→ Children find sugar ....

e. My remark was an accident.
→ My remark was ....

10. Remplacez 'right' par un *question tag* dans *Everybody likes cake, right?* (l. 1).

....

11. Dites ce que *'shall we?'* (l. 3) reprend.

....

12. Circle the correct proposition.

a. Not everybody *like/likes* coconut.
b. *Has/have* everybody got *his/their* square?
c. All Australians *like/likes* Lamington.
d. *Every Australian like/every Australian likes/every Australians like* Lamington.

13. Fill in the blanks with the appropriate question tag.

a. Pass me the coffee, ...?
b. You have made Lamington, ...?
c. You don't have to add jam, ...?
d. She never eats cake, ...?
e. I'm very greedy, ...?
f. The cake is barely edible, ...?
g. Everybody likes cake, ...?
h. Nobody hated the cake, ...?
i. New Zealand invented Lamington, ...?

14. Entourez le bon *tag* dans cette phrase prononcée avec énervement, ironie ou colère.

New Zealand invented Lamington, *did they/didn't it?/did it?/didn't they?*

UNIT 10

15. Entourez l'intonation qu'il faut prendre pour prononcer ces deux phrases (montante ou descendante).
a. Lamington cake requires jam, doesn't it? (I'm not sure)   ↑ ↓
b. Lamington doesn't require jam, does it? (I'm sure)   ↑ ↓

16. Match each sentence with its end.
a. My father loved coconut, and ●   ● **1.** neither did I.
b. You did not like coffee, ●   ● **2.** I think so.
c. Is the cake burning? ●   ● **3.** so did I.
d. Is Lamington Australian? ●   ● **4.** Yes, please.
e. Would you like a piece of cake? ●   ● **5.** I hope not.

17. Remettez les mots de ces traductions dans l'ordre.
a. Je suppose que tu n'es pas au courant :
know/I/suppose/you/don't ....

b. Ne mangeons pas trop :
too/eat/us/not/much/let ....

c. Il m'a demandé de ne pas ajouter de confiture :
add/not/jam/asked/any/to/me/he ....

d. Tout le monde n'aime pas le Lamington :
Lamington/likes/not/everybody ....

e. Le gâteau n'était pas assez gros :
enough/cake/the/was/big/not ....

18. Correct the mistakes in these sentences, if any.
a. Not only do I love coconut, but I also cook it very well.
....

b. The ten first squares of Lamington disappeared within minutes.
....

c. I can't remember what are the ingredients.
....

d. We used the last two duck eggs to bake the cake. They were twice as bigger as hen's eggs.
....

e. I thought it would be too big a cake for us to eat, but the cake was actually too little.
....

f. Your advices were good; we needed twice as much cakes.
....

UNIT 10

19. Fill in the blanks with either *some* or *any*.

a. Wow, this is .... cake you baked!
b. It's not just .... car, it's a Bentley, Sir!
c. Would you like .... cake? Of course you do!
d. .... type of coffee will do if you don't have time to make Irish coffee.

20. Fill in the blanks with *from*, *in*, *to*, *on* or *over*.

a. My best friend is married .... an Australian guy.
b. Aussies and Kiwis fight .... Lamington's origin.
c. The answer .... your question is easy.
d. There has been an increase .... the demand for cocoa.
e. Congratulations .... making such a delicious cake.
f. This glove will protect you .... the heat.

21. Trouvez l'homophone des mots suivants dans le texte.

a. rite: ....
b. hole: ....
c. pear: ....

22. Entourez les deux affirmations fausses.

a. Le ow de *bowl* et de *powder* se prononce [a-o].
b. 1901 se dit 'nineteen o one' [naïn'tin o^{eu} 'oueunn].
c. *National* se prononce en deux syllabes ['nachn^{eul}].
d. *Indulge* rime avec *huge*.

23. Circle the number of syllables you can hear in the following words.

a. temperature   2 – 3 – 4
b. chocolate   1 – 2 – 3
c. cocoa   1 – 2 – 3

24. Entourez le mot dont le *a* ne se prononce pas.

PAIR/COCOA/CLAIM/COMPANION/EXTRA

25. Trouvez la seule affirmation exacte.

a. *Dessert* et *desert* se prononcent tous deux ['dèz^{eu}t].
b. *Tangy* se prononce ['tandji].
c. Le nom *advice* se prononce [^{eu}'dvaïss] alors que le verbe *to advise* se prononce [^{eu}'dvaïz].

26. Les mots suivants ont été classés selon la prononciation de leur *s*. Dites si ce classement est exact ou s'il comporte des erreurs (précisez lesquelles, le cas échéant).

[ch]: **s**ugar, **s**ure, expan**s**ion, ti**ss**ue, **s**ensual, pre**ss**ure
[j]:   clo**s**ure, A**s**ia, mea**s**ure, lei**s**ure
[z]:   de**s**ert, po**ss**ess, clum**s**y
[ss]: ba**s**ic, relea**s**e, preci**s**ely, di**s**appear

108

UNIT 10

27. Classez les mots suivants en fonction de la prononciation de leur *-ate* final.

CHOCOLATE/DELICATE/TO DESICCATE/
TO GRATE/DESPERATE/PASSIONATE/
CLIMATE/TO CONGRATULATE

[ᵉᵘT]	[ÈÏT]

28. Chassez l'intrus (prononciation du *-ed*).

a. melted/coated/iced/desiccated
b. invented/dissolved/presented/grated
c. shaped/named/concerned/dissolved

VOCABULARY INTERLUDE

29. Remettez les lettres dans l'ordre pour reconstituer les traductions suivantes.

a. pâte à tartiner :   chocolate DASPER ....
b. pépite de chocolat : chocolate PHIC ....
c. chocolat noir :   KRAD .... chocolate

30. Trouvez les lettres manquantes dans ces traductions (types de noix).

a. noisette   H __ __ELNUT
b. cacahuète   __ ANUT
c. marron   __HE __TNUT
d. noix commune   W__ __ NUT

31. En prenant la dernière lettre de chaque mot à deviner en a. et b., vous trouverez le mot manquant dans les traductions c. et d.

c. vanilla .... (gousse de vanille)
d. coffee .... (grain de café)

a. Place where you buy things   __ __ __ __
Number indicating 'none'   __ __ __ __
Not happy   __ __ __
b. Place where you drink beers   __ __ __
Not the truth   __ __ __
Greek cheese   __ __ __ __
Nine + one   __ __ __

UNIT 10

32. Chassez l'intrus.

DECAF/INSTANT/LOOSE/HALF AND HALF/JAVA/JOE/BLACK

33. Match every way of drinking to their meaning in French.

a. to nurse
b. to sip
c. to slurp
d. to wash down
e. to swig

1. boire en accompagnement d'un plat
2. boire en faisant du bruit
3. boire à grands traits, « siffler »
4. siroter
5. boire lentement, prendre son temps pour boire

34. Complétez les espaces par *cake* ou *nut*.

a. You can't win both ways. You can't have your .... and eat it too.
b. There are many things wrong in this recipe, but in a .... shell, you need more chocolate and coconut.
c. This problem is very complex. It's a tough .... to crack.
d. Getting the manager position was already good, but the pay rise was the icing on the ....
e. This book is a best seller. It sells like hot .... s.
f. He went .... s when he heard his football team had lost.

35. Circle the right proposition.

a. Something almost too good to be true is:
   1. a golden cake
   2. a coconut
   3. a chocolate box

b. When someone is embarrassed about doing something wrong, they have .... on their face:
   1. jam
   2. chocolate spread
   3. cake

c. Means « réagis, atterris, réveille-toi ! »
   1. Wake up and break the eggs!
   2. Wake up and smell the coffee!
   3. Wake up and bake a cake!

UNIT 10

BACK TO WORK – LAUGH AND LEARN

36. Lisez le texte ci-dessous, séparez les mots dans les affirmations a-g, puis dites si elles sont vraies ou fausses.

There are some weird coffee traditions around the world. In Finland and Sweden for example, people drink *kaffeost*, coffee containing small squares of cheese in it. In some countries like Vietnam and Hungary, people mix raw eggs and black coffee. The practice is quite old. It goes out and comes back into fashion now and then, even in Europe or the United States. Writer Victor Hugo already had the habit of drinking his coffee with two raw eggs in it. Today the trend is popular with those who work out a lot. But there is a more surprising coffee tradition from Indonesia, Brazil, and Thailand, that uses coffee beans picked out from the faeces of various animals before they are roasted. These coffees are among the most expensive in the world. The most recent coffee innovation comes from Australia, where the Commonwealth Scientific and Industrial Research Organisation launched broccoli coffee in 2018 – powdered broccoli is simply added to your latte. They are hoping it will help people consume more vitamins from greens and prevent food wastage as well since they are going to use unsaleable broccoli.

VRAI   FAUX

a. Weird means 'strange'.
b. In Austria there is a coffee made with broccoli.
c. In some countries, coffee beans are collected from animals' poo.
d. Broccoli coffee consists of powdered broccoli added to black coffee.
e. Mixing raw eggs and coffee is not a new thing invented by workout addicts.
f. Broccoli coffee is going to use vegetables meant to be thrown to the bin.
g. People who exercise are putting cheese in their coffee.

37. Lisez attentivement ces citations, puis entourez l'affirmation fausse.

'Chocolate is nature's way of making up for Mondays'. *(Anon)*

'Only Irish coffee provides in a single glass all four essential food groups: alcohol, caffeine, sugar, and fat.' *(Alex Levine)*

'Strength is the capacity to break a Hershey bar into four pieces with your bare hands and then eat just one of the pieces.' *(Judith Viorst)*

'My therapist told me the way to achieve true inner peace is to finish what I start. So far today, I've finished two bags of M&Ms and a chocolate cake. I feel better already.' *(Dave Barry)*

a. Alex Levine is being ironic about the nutritionally balanced profile of Irish coffee.
b. Chocolate makes Mondays worse.
c. Dave Barry has found a sense of self-fulfillment in chocolate.
d. It takes a lot of self-control not to eat more than one square of chocolate.

UNIT 10

38. Reliez chaque début de proverbe ou citation à la suite qui lui correspond, puis devinez la signification des termes mentionnés sous le tableau.

a. 'Even clever hens sometimes lay ●
b. 'A rotten coconut in a heap ●
c. 'All you need is love. But a little chocolate now ●
d. 'Only the man who is not hungry ●
e. 'I could give up chocolate but ●

● **1.** spoils the wholesome ones.' (Swahili proverb)
● **2.** says the coconut has a hard shell.' (Ethiopian proverb)
● **3.** their eggs among nettles.' (Danish poverb)
● **4.** I'm not a quitter.' (Lora Brody)
● **5.** and then doesn't hurt.' (Charles M. Schulz)

a. I mean 'rusé/intelligent' ....
b. I mean 'pourri(e)' ....
c. I mean 'coque, coquille' ....
d. I mean 'orties' ....
e. I mean 'stop' ....
f. I mean 'qui baisse facilement les bras' ....

39. Les mots en gras sont placés dans la mauvaise phrase, remettez-les à leur place.

a. 'Drink coffee while it's hot enough to make you **take** → .... but let the chocolate cool.' (Sicilian proverb)
b. 'The most dangerous food is a **whiskey** → .... cake.' (American proverb)
c. 'What butter and **wedding** → .... will not cure there's no cure for.' (Irish proverb)
d. 'He who selects coconut with great **hips** → .... ends up getting a bad coconut.' (Swahili proverb)
e. 'You can't **swear** → .... the milk back from the coffee.' (Jamaican proverb)
f. 'A moment on the lips, a lifetime on the **care** → ....' (English proverb)

40. Entourez la signification du mot *shag* (très familier, vulgaire) dans cette citation d'Eddie Izzard plaisantant sur les publicités pour le café.

a. to smile like an idiot
b. to have sex
c. to become rich

"Oh, look at that! Those two people like it, and they're shagging!" That's what happens, isn't it? Shagging sells everything! That's it, there's an advert for coffee. You come around, "Cup of coffee? – Ooh, let's shag!"

UNIT 10

END-OF-CHAPTER TEST

41. Translate these sentences into English.

1. L'acidité du café noir est contrebalancée par la douceur du sucre brun et de la crème fouettée.

2. Mes enfants ont le bec sucré et ne peuvent pas résister à ce gâteau au chocolat fondu. Nous non plus.

3. Les deux premières fois que j'ai fait du Lamington, je l'ai raté. J'avais acheté de la noix de coco râpée lambda qui manquait de croquant.

4. Le gâteau est tout plat, c'est bizarre. Tu as oublié d'ajouter la levure à la pâte, non ?

5. Ma sœur prétend que le nom de ce gâteau vient de la reine Victoria. Je ne pense pas.

UNIT 11

1. Now, will you succumb to the sweet temptation of Southern soul
2. food with peach cobbler? That's a no-brainer! Peach cobbler is
3. a baked dish of peaches topped with a delicious buttery crust.
4. Peach cobbler is both foolproof – the easiest baking recipe there
5. is – and terrific: there's no resisting the melt-in-the mouth texture
6. of the gooey peaches, the soft crust, and the faint aroma of
7. cinnamon. Many people think, wrongly so, that cobbler comes
8. down to a kind of crumble. The two desserts are quite distinct,
9. not only because the composition and texture of the dough
10. is different, but also because cobbler is not crumbled on top
11. but layered in irregular circles – by the way, cobbler is called
12. so because the coarse and irregular dough crust on top looks
13. like cobblestones. Although cobblers can be made with almost
14. any fresh fruit, typical cobblers are made with peaches. This
15. dessert is a classic in the Southern United States, particularly
16. in the sunny peach-producing state of Georgia – it is with good
17. reason that Georgia's nickname is 'the peach state.' For this
18. recipe, it is better to use fresh peaches if they are in season,
19. but if they aren't, good-quality canned ones will do the job.
20. Peach cobbler tastes its best served lukewarm, accompanied
21. by vanilla ice cream.

PEACH COBBLER

INGREDIENTS

4 TO 6 SERVINGS:

- 120 g of unsalted butter, melted
- 140 g of flour
- 300 g of sugar
- 1 tablespoon of baking powder
- 1 pinch of salt
- 250 ml of milk
- 12 peaches, sliced
- 1 tablespoon of lemon juice
- 1 or 2 teaspoons of ground cinnamon (to taste)

1. Pour the melted butter in your baking dish.

2. Combine the flour, half the sugar, the baking powder, and the salt. Then add the milk, stirring until you get a thick batter. Pour the batter in the buttered dish (do not stir).

3. Mix the remaining sugar, the peach slices, and the lemon juice, and boil the mixture over high heat, continuously stirring. Pour it over the batter (do not stir). Sprinkle with cinnamon.

4. Bake at 190° C for 45 minutes, until golden brown. Leave to cool for a bit and serve lukewarm.

UNIT 11

QUESTIONS AROUND THE TEXT

1. Correct the mistakes in this summary about cobbler.

Peach cobbler is a typical finger-food dessert. It's very popular in the state of Georgia, which is hardly surprising since

Georgia is famous for growing prime-quality peaches. Cobbler is a kind of pie with a top layer of crunchy sweet peaches.

It is characterized by the overwhelming presence of cinnamon. What is great with cobbler is that it is easy to prepare

and you needn't use fresh peaches if they are off-season. Cobbler is better eaten straight out from the oven so as to

contrast with the coldness of ice cream it is accompanied by.

2. Reliez ces adjectifs à leur définition.

a. wet and sticky (in a sugary, positive way)
b. neither warm, nor cold
c. fantastic, great
d. that you cannot miss or spoil
e. discreet, evanescent

1. lukewarm (l. 20)
2. foolproof (l. 4)
3. gooey (l. 6)
4. faint (l. 6)
5. terrific (l. 5)

3. Fill in the blanks using *terrific* or *terrible*.

a. Jim had an accident, what .... news!
b. I have found a new job. That's .... !

4. Circle the right proposition.

a. A cobbler is a dessert but also the name for a:
   1. jewellery maker
   2. hat maker
   3. shoe maker

b. A no-brainer (l. 2) comes from the word *brain* ('*cerveau*') and it means
   1. an easy decision to make
   2. a dilemma
   3. a joke

c. To melt (l. 5) means:
   1. to turn cold
   2. to become solid
   3. to become liquid

d. 'Comes down to' (l. 7-8) can be replaced by:
   1. is nothing more than
   2. is nothing like

UNIT 11

5. Entourez les expressions synonymes de *will do the job* (l. 19).
a. will fit the bill
b. will do the trick
c. will suit
d. will ring a bell

6. Entourez les constructions compatibles.
a. I need .... peaches. *a few – a little – any – some – five – Ø – few*
b. Have you got .... honey? *Ø – enough – any – some – much – many*
c. We have .... news from her. *no – little – few – some – a little – enough*
d. There isn't .... sugar in the recipe. *enough – no – any – a few – little*

7. Fill in the blanks with either *it* or *Ø*.
a. As .... was expected, they brought some cobbler for us to taste.
b. They took .... for granted that you would use peaches. As I told .... you, you can make cobbler with apricots.
c. This peach variety is not sweet enough for me to cook ....
d. As .... happened last year, your chutney was a delight. I find .... amazing that you cook so well.
e. As I see ...., cobblers are better with nutmeg. I love .... when you use nutmeg instead of cinnamon.
f. Your cobbler is dry, you cooked it longer than .... was necessary.
g. Making cobbler was not as easy as I had expected ....

8. Complete the following rephrasings.
There's no resisting (l. 5) = You .... resist = It is .... resist = It is …resist…..

9. À partir de l'expression *there's no resisting* employé l. 5, traduisez les phrases suivantes.
a. There's no denying your cobbler is better than mine.
....
b. There's no knowing when the peaches will be ripe.
....

10. En vous inspirant de l'expression *wrongly so* (l. 7), formez un synonyme de *with good reason* (l. 16-17).
....

117

UNIT 11

11. Fill in the blanks with either *most*, *each*, *every*, or *all*.

a. .... peaches are juicy.
b. I eat cobbler .... single day.
c. I have a peach in .... hand.
d. .... of the peaches were off.
e. .... of us – one by one – was given a peach.
f. .... cobblers were baked in my oven.

12. Complétez les blancs par *in, at, out, on, to, of,* ou *with*.

a. Thanks .... you, I now know how to make cobbler.
b. Because .... the rain, we can't pick peaches today.
c. I had no peaches .... hand, so I put pears in my cobbler.
d. I called them first, ... of respect for them.
e. Congratulations .... getting a new job! Let's drink .... your success!
f. The components .... cobbler are inexpensive.
g. The dessert abounds .... sugar, but it's got a tangy taste .... it nonetheless.

13. Circle the right proposition.

a. Georgia is famous *worldwise – worldwide* for peaches.
b. I'm going to take some more cobbler. You can do *likewise – likewide*.
c. Jack has a *southern – south* accent.
d. I live in the *southern – south of* London.

14. Complétez le tableau.

DISCOURS DIRECT	DISCOURS INDIRECT
a. Betty: 'I left Dublin last year.'	Betty said ....
b. Henry: 'I will pick up the peaches tomorrow.'	Henry said ....
c. Jim: 'I can help you.'	Jim said ....

UNIT 11

15. Remettez les mots dans l'ordre pour reconstituer le discours indirect correspondant à chacune de ces phrases.

a. 'I was wrong.' → *been/he/that/wrong/had/admitted/he*

b. 'You should not put on too much cinnamon.' → *much/us/cinnamon/on/too/not/he/use/advised/to*

c. 'How about going out for some cobbler?' → *Cobbler/go/she/some/that/we/suggested/for/out*

d. 'Where are the peaches coming from?' → *peaches/wonder/from/where/are/I/coming/the*

e. 'What does "melt" mean?' → *meant/what/asked/melt/we*

16. Complete the following rephrasings from a. to d. and give the direct speech from e. to g.

a. 'What's your favourite fruit?' Tell me ....

b. 'Do they need more peaches?' I wonder ....

c. 'Where is the butter?' Do you know ....

d. 'How ripe are the peaches?' I asked him ....

e. '.............................. ?' He asked me when they would visit.

f. '.............................. ?' He wondered whether I had bought peaches or not.

g. '.............................. !' He told me not to eat ice cream.

17. Chassez l'intrus (prononciation).
CRUMB – THUMB – CRUMBLE – SUCCUMB – DUMB

18. Corrigez les affirmations inexactes.

a. *dough* rime avec *enough*.

b. *gooey* rime avec *way*.

c. *cinnamon* se prononce ['tchinam^(eu)n].

d. *vanilla* se prononce [^(veu)'nil^(eu)].

e. *lukewarm* se prononce [l**ou'**kouôm].

UNIT 11

19. Trouvez dans le texte les homophones des mots suivants.
a. course: ....(l. ....)
b. aunt: ....(l. ....)

20. Entourez les trois mots mal accentués parmi cette liste de mots contenant des suffixes dits « non neutres » (affectant la place de l'accent par rapport au mot racine).
SATIS'FACTORY, COM'MUNICATE, A'PPROPRIATE, TEMP'TATION, AM'BITIOUS, PO'SSIBILITY, FA'MILIAR, CREDI'BILITY, PSY'CHOLOGY, FI'NANCIAL, 'COMPOSITION, PHO'TOGRAPHY, VEGE'TARIAN, RUDI'MENTARY, COMPA'NION, CA'NADIAN, DE'LICIOUS, I'RREGULAR

VOCABULARY INTERLUDE

21. Circle the correct proposition.
a. 'Fruits du verger' are *meadow – orchard – field* fruit.
b. I am an acidic type of fruit. My stalks are consumed in jams and cobblers. I am *sorrel – rhubarb – cranberry*.
c. *abricotts – apricots – apriccots* are small orange-coloured fruit. They can replace peaches in cobblers.
d. Bartlett is a famous variety of *pears – peaches – apples*.
e. 'Beurre non salé' is *sweet butter – plain butter – staple butter*.

22. Détachez les mots au bon endroit, puis associez-les à leur traduction française.
SCOOPWAFFLECONESORBETSHERBETGRANITAITALIANICE
GELATOPOPSICLEFROZENYOGHURTSUNDAETOPPING

a. glace à l'eau sur bâtonnet ....
b. cône (gaufré) ....
c. coupe glacée ....
d. glace à mi-chemin entre le sorbet et la crème glacée ....
e. yaourt glacé ....
f. boule ....
g. glace très crémeuse à l'italienne ....
h. sorbet ....
i. nappage ....

UNIT 11

23. Reliez chaque début de proverbe à sa suite, puis devinez comment se traduisent les expressions données en A et B.

- **a.** She is very nice. She's sugar and
- **b.** The skin on her face is like porcelain. It's all peaches
- **c.** They divorced last year. Their marriage had gone
- **d.** Be careful not to trade off the orchard for
- **e.** Oh, thank you darling. You're a real

- **1.** an apple.
- **2.** pear-shaped.
- **3.** peach.
- **4.** and cream.
- **5.** spice.

A. tourner au vinaigre ....

B. être un amour ....

24. Trouvez les lettres manquantes dans ces mots désignant des types de sucre.

a.	sucre cristallisé	*Granu___ted sugar*
b.	sucre en poudre	*Cas_ _r sugar, _ _ _fectioner's sugar, _cing sugar, powde_ _d sugar*
c.	sucre en grains (ou sucre perlé)	*_ear_ sugar*
d.	types de sucres bruns	*_ane sugar, Demera_ _sugar, Mus_ _ vado sugar*
e.	mélasse	*M_lass_ _*

25. Circle the correct word.

To take out a *lump – limp – lamp* of sugar from a sugar bowl, you use sugar *prongs – tongs – pokers.*

26. Fill in the blanks with either *sugar, honey, candy* or *cookie*.

a. Anna is a very strong person, she's a tough ....

b. The U.S.A. have always been seen as a land of milk and ....; a land where you could make it.

c. Beating their team was so easy; as easy as taking .... from a baby!

d. If you .... coat bad news, you're making it sound positive although it's not.

e. 'You can catch more flies with .... than with vinegar' means that sweet words are the easiest way to win people over.

f. A .... daddy is a rich older man who buys a young woman things, in exchange for sexual favors.

UNIT 11

27. Placez ces termes alimentaires dans le tableau.
ARUGULA, CHIPS, CILANTRO, COOKIES, ZUCCHINI, CRISPS, EGGPLANT, GRANOLA, SWEETS

BRITISH	AMERICAN	FRANÇAIS
a. aubergine	....	aubergine
b. coriander	....	coriandre
c. biscuits	....	biscuits
d.	candies	bonbons
e.	fries	frites
f.	chips	chips
g. courgette	....	courgette
h. muesli	....	muesli
i. rocket	....	roquette

BACK TO WORK – LAUGH AND LEARN

28. Correct the mistakes in the following text, and then place the words provided below in the appropriate a-d statements that are about the text.

Based on the asumption that vanilla is the defaut flavour that most people chose when buying ice cream, the word

....

vanilla has came to mean basic, ordinary, standard. It can carry negative conotations and mean plane, unadventurous,

....

and borring. The word is particulaly used in sexual contexts. The misionnary position for exemple will be labelled as

....

vanilla, and sex that does not envolve any 'naughty' things such like fetichism or S&M may be considerred by some as

....

'*vanilla* sex'. As for the word 'peach', it is often used as a metaphor for womens' buttocs or private parts, and by

....

extansion it can also refer to sexual intercoarse.

....

BEHAVIOUR – KINKY – BREASTS – WITHIN – DULL

a. The word *vanilla* can be synonymous with ...., monotonous.

b. Women's behinds, not .... as often thought, are sometimes referred to as their peaches.

c. The missionary position is considered the opposite of ....

d. Vanilla sex can be defined as conventional sexual .... a society.

UNIT 11

29. En vous aidant des indices fournis entre parenthèses, remettez les lettres dans l'ordre dans ces citations.

a. 'Pears can just KUCF FOF .... (go away, slang) too. 'Cause they're ESORGOGU .... (beautiful) little beasts, but they're PIRE .... (mature) for half an hour, and you're never there.' (Eddie Izzard)

b. 'In Hollywood, the women are all peaches. It makes one GNOL .... for (desire, want) an apple LYNOSACALOCI .... (once in a while, now and then).' (W. Somerset Maugham)

c. 'When peaches flower and PIREN .... (to become ripe), days and nights have the same GNELTH .... (longueur).' (Corsican proverb)

30. Entourez la ou les expressions signifiant la même idée que ce proverbe Hausa. *'Even sugar itself may spoil a good dish.'*

a. too much of a good thing
b. to kick the bucket
c. to beat about the bush
d. to over-egg the pudding
e. to bark up the wrong tree

31. À une lettre près, les mots en gras sont inexacts, corrigez l'erreur.

a. 'Georgia on my **mend** ....' (catchphrase originating from Ray Charles's song)

b. 'Bless your **earth** ....' (Southern American phrase, usually used after or before a negative comment)

END-OF-CHAPTER TEST

32. Translate these sentences into English

1. Je me demande où sont la muscade et la cannelle. Elle a dit qu'elle les avait rangées dans le placard du haut.

2. On ne peut pas nier que c'est l'idéal quand on peut se procurer des fruits de saison bien tendres, ça tombe sous le sens.

3. Elle a demandé, à juste titre, si je pourrais marcher longtemps sur des pavés avec ces chaussures.

4. Ce cobbler surmonté de poires bien collantes de sucre sera d'enfer servi tiède avec de la glace.

5. Tu es un amour, tu m'as ramené de bons abricots du marché. Si j'ai le temps, j'en ferai de la compote, sinon un cobbler.

UNIT 12

We will end our gourmet escapade with a light but mouth-watering Scottish dessert called Cranachan. Like most people, you may not be aware of the fact that raspberries thrive in colder climates, but Scotland is famous for its sweet and tasty raspberries. Cranachan gathers all of Scotland's agricultural assets: nice and tart raspberries, crunchy oats, smooth cream, sweet honey, and invigorating whisky. It is a beautifully layered trifle served in tall glass bowls that is as pleasing to the eyes as it is to the taste buds. This dessert is not costly – it's Scotland after all – and it can be a last-minute surprise, ready in under fifteen minutes. The only thing to be careful about is that frozen or canned raspberries tend to be soggy or lacking in juiciness and flavour, so make sure you use fresh ones. You can place all the ingredients on the table and leave it to your guests to combine their bowls themselves, as is customary in Nessie's country.

CRANACHAN

INGREDIENTS

SERVINGS 4:
- 60 g of oats
- 400 g of fresh raspberries
- 400 g of full-fat cream or mascarpone
- 6 tablespoons of liquid honey
- 90 ml of whisky

1. Toast the oats in a frying pan until browned and leave to cool.

2. In a bowl, lightly crush the raspberries (but keep 12 to 16 whole ones for the topping). In another bowl, mix the cream (or mascarpone), 3 tablespoons of honey, and 45 ml of whisky. Whip until the mixture thickens a little.

3. In another bowl, mix the remaining honey and whisky.

4. Layer in glasses: raspberries, oats, cream mixture, raspberries, oats, cream mixture (in that order). Put a few whole raspberries on top, drizzle with the honey-whisky mix, and enjoy!

UNIT 12

QUESTIONS AROUND THE TEXT

1. Replace each underlined word with one item from the word bank provided below.

less than – all the qualities – main – avoid using – subtle – ground – encapsulates – well-known – necessity – climatic

Cranachan is a light and 1. <u>refined</u> .... dessert from Scotland, which is 2. <u>famous</u> .... for producing top-quality raspberries. The Scottish 3. <u>land</u> .... has indeed the perfect 4. <u>weather</u> .... conditions since the precious berries like the cold. Cranachan 5. <u>summarizes</u> .... Scotland on its own as it contains the 6. <u>principle</u> .... foods the country is good at producing. The dessert has 7. <u>everything going for it</u> .... as it is not expensive to make and it is ready in 8. <u>under</u> .... fifteen minutes. The only absolute 9. <u>requirement</u> .... to make the perfect Cranachan is to 10. <u>keep away from</u> .... frozen fruit and use fresh raspberries.

2. The words in *green* (used in the text) have been placed in the wrong sentences. Put them back in the sentences they belong to.

a. If you are *soggy* → .... something, you know about it and take it into account.
b. The *costly* → .... are specific cells on the tongue that make things flavourful.
c. An ingredient that is *asset* → .... contains too much water and has lost its freshness.
d. An *aware of* → .... is an advantage, something that is in your favour.
e. *taste buds* → .... is a sweet edible substance secreted by bees.
f. If something is *honey* → .... , it is expensive.

3. Circle the name(s) of anyone who is not aware of what Cranachan is.

Adam is clueless about what it is
– Olivia has no truck with it – Kim has no idea what it is

4. Retrouvez la traduction anglaise de ces mots dans la grille (mots du texte et de la recette).

a. prospérer, s'épanouir
b. réunir, rassembler
c. flocons d'avoine
d. épaissir
e. arroser, asperger
f. surgelés
g. surnom affectif du monstre du Loch Ness
h. dessert anglais très commun avec de la crème et des fruits

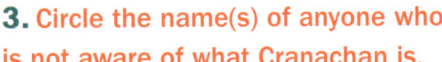

F	T	O	T	R	I	F	L	E	B	T	T
U	R	H	N	Z	M	D	N	S	M	H	E
B	N	O	C	T	H	R	I	V	E	I	G
T	O	B	Z	K	C	W	X	Z	B	C	A
A	A	O	G	E	S	Q	H	G	R	K	B
A	T	Z	A	P	N	A	N	M	T	E	N
E	S	F	T	S	G	S	E	U	N	N	M
W	X	O	H	T	V	N	S	V	V	O	J
N	E	R	E	T	W	S	S	U	V	I	U
I	B	H	R	M	G	A	I	S	Z	U	F
L	D	R	I	Z	Z	L	E	R	D	A	K
Y	N	F	U	C	O	H	H	F	B	D	Y

UNIT 12

5. En associant correctement ces lettres ou ces groupes de lettres, vous pourrez trouver les mots utilisés dans le texte et évoqués dans les énigmes.

a. I mean *acidic* but in a pleasant way: ....
b. I am usually used to make porridge: ....
c. I am a type of dessert but I also mean *a thing of no consequence*: ....

```
    TA    O
IFL   TR    AT
  S   RT    E
```

6. Chassez l'intrus.

MOUTH-WATERING, DELIGHTFUL, SCRUMMY, RUN OF THE MILL, YUMMY, PALATABLE, SCRUMPTIOUS

7. Complétez ce tableau.

COUNTRY	NATIONALITY	NOUN
a. Scotland	Scottish	....
b. Poland	Polish	....
c.	Swedish	....
d.	Dutch	....
e. Turkey	....	....

8. Entourez le cliché auquel fait référence le commentaire *'It's Scotland after all.'* (l. 9-10)

a. Les Écossais sont riches.
b. Les Écossais sont radins.
c. Les Écossais sont très maigres.

9. Reliez chaque début d'énoncé à sa suite.

a. Cranachan is a time- ●   ● **1.** looking men.
b. The list of ingredients was never- ●   ● **2.** growing country.
c. Scotland is a raspberry- ●   ● **3.** saving dessert when you're busy.
d. The Scots are good- ●   ● **4.** ending for this recipe.

10. Écrivez en toutes lettres les éléments en gras, puis dites comment les pourcentages se prononcent (entre crochets).

'Most people' (l. 2) could mean **90 %** .... [.....................................] of people, as well as **92.5 %** .... [.....................................] or **'neuf sur dix'**: ..../.........

UNIT 12

11. Dites comment se prononcent (oralement, non phonétiquement) l'adresse e-mail et le numéro de téléphone mentionnés dans l'échange suivant.

– Your Cranachan was amazing. Where did you get the raspberries?
– We picked them ourselves at Barrie's farm this afternoon. Look, here is his brochure.
– Thanks, RASPICK@co.uk, phone number 09 08 55 93 40
....

12. Fill in the blanks with *by, to, on, about, at, in,* or *of*

a. I'm crazy .... raspberries, and Scotland produces the best .... the world.
b. Cranachan is the perfect dessert if you're .... a budget and .... a tight schedule.
c. Make yourself .... home, but go easy .... the whisky!
d. You did not arrive .... time, but you still arrived .... time for dessert.
e. Cranachan! How kind .... you. I haven't had any .... years. It will remind me .... my homeland.
f. Be kind .... your sister. She's not keen .... cooking like you.
g. The raspberries should be .... season .... the end of the month.

13. Corrigez l'erreur d'adjectif contenue dans chacune de ces phrases.

a. Some Japanese chefs cook alive fish. ....
b. An afraid dog can bite. ....
c. Don't disturb an asleep dog. ....
d. An ill person can be contagious. ....
e. An alone child can get bored. ....

14. L'intensificateur *very* n'est pas utilisable dans les phrases suivantes (qui sont donc incorrectes, ce que signale le *). Corrigez-les en remplaçant *very* par un des mots suivants.

QUITE – SOUND – DEEPLY – GREATLY – WIDE - MUCH – WELL

a. Liam is very* .... asleep but Fiona is very* .... awake.
b. My sister is a very* .... loved woman.
c. Your cat died? That's very* .... awful!
d. My brother was very* .... taller than I was.
e. I'm very* .... in love with Alan.
f. This man's IQ is very* .... above average.

UNIT 12

15. Translate the following sentences into French (be careful about the adverb 'very').

a. Cranachan was my very first Scottish food.

....

b. He made the recipe before my very eyes.

....

16. Put the verbs in brackets in the passive form.

a. Thousands of Cranachans (eat) .... every day.

b. Cranachan (invent) .... in Scotland in the 18th century.

c. Fresh raspberries (deliver) .... next week.

d. The raspberries (pick up) .... It's done!

e. Cranachan (make) .... by Paul as we are speaking.

17. Remettez les éléments dans l'ordre pour former des phrases passives correctes puis proposez une traduction.

a. of/spoken/parts/in/Scotland/Gaelic/still/is/some

....

b. century/said/to date/the 18th/Cranachan is/back to

....

c. that you/I was/were Scottish/told

....

d. nowhere to/raspberries are/the/be found

....

18. Separate the words properly to form the English translation of these sentences.

a. anewvarietyofraspberrieshasbeendiscovered: une nouvelle variété de framboises a été découverte

....

b. afullbasketofraspberrieshasbeengiventous: un plein panier de framboises nous a été offert

....

c. weweregivenhalfabasketofraspberries: on nous a donné un demi-panier de framboises

....

19. Mettez ces phrases à la forme passive.

a. Someone will find out your secret.

....

b. People had to deal with the problem.

....

UNIT 12

20. Convert these sentences so as to put the emphasis on the object in a. and on the recipient in b.

ACCENT SUR L'OBJET	ACCENT SUR LE DESTINATAIRE
a.	**a.** We will be sent a postcard from Scotland.
b. A vintage whisky was given to me.	**b.** ....

21. Reliez chaque début de phrase à sa suite.

- **a.** We had my raspberries
- **b.** We would like to make him
- **c.** The farmer will get
- **d.** The raspberries are dusty. They need

- **1.** rinse our raspberries.
- **2.** rinsing.
- **3.** rinsed; I didn't do it myself.
- **4.** the raspberries rinsed before delivery.

22. Circle the number of syllables you can hear in these words.

- **a.** raspberry: 2 – 3
- **b.** customary: 3 – 4
- **c.** immediately: 4 – 5 – 6

23. Trouvez dans la liste de mots fournis ceux qui correspondent aux devinettes.

CUSTOMARY, GUEST, ESCAPADE, HONEY, BUDS, GOURMET, OBEY, PLACE, SURVEY, GREY, SHEPHERD, BERRY, TART, RASPBERRY, BLADE, DECADE, UNDER

- **a.** Mon *p* ne se prononce pas : ....
- **b.** J'ai un homophone qui signifie « enterrer » : ....
- **c.** Mon *t* final ne se prononce pas : ....
- **d.** Mon *u* ne se prononce pas : ....
- **e.** Mon *ey* se prononce comme celui de *money* : ....
- **f.** Notre *u* se prononce comme dans *cup* : ....
- **g.** Je suis l'homonyme d'un type de poisson blanc : ....

24. Trouvez le point de prononciation commun entre ces mots.

PSYCHOLOGY – CUPBOARD – RECEIPT – PSEUDO – RASPBERRY – PNEUMONIA

UNIT 12

25. Entourez la bonne prononciation.

   a. soggy
      1. ['sodji]
      2. ['sogi]
   b. liquid
      1. ['likouid]
      2. ['likid]
   c. escapade
      1. ['èsk^eu pad]
      2. ['èsk^eu pèïd]

26. Dites si les affirmations suivantes sont vraies ou fausses.

                                                           VRAI   **FAUX**

a. Le **t** se prononce de la même façon dans *gourmet (l. 1)* et *asset (l. 6)*.

b. Le **i** se prononce [i] dans *thrive, drizzle, mixture* et *climate*.

c. Le **u** de *buds* et le **o** de *honey* se prononcent de la même façon.

27. Les voyelles de syllabes non accentuées se prononcent généralement [^eu] (son très bref). Entourez ce son dans les mots suivants.

'pizza, in'gredient, 'famous, com'puter, 'climate, 'Scotland, 'chocolate, 'cinema, 'instant, 'children, 'husband, A'merican, a'fraid, a'gain, 'energy, po'tato, 'accident, ba'nana

VOCABULARY INTERLUDE

28. Placez chaque proposition à l'endroit adéquat pour former un nom de fruit rouge.

BLUE – BLACK – CRAN – STRAW – GOOSE

   a. fraise : .....berry
   b. myrtille : .....berry
   c. canneberge : .....berry
   d. groseille : .....berry
   e. mûre : .....berry

29. Find the missing letters in these translations.

   a. cassis : BLAC_ _ _ _ RANT
   b. grenade : PO_ _ GRA_ _ TE
   c. cerise : _ _ _ RRY

30. Entourez la bonne proposition.
Le porridge d'avoine s'appelle :
   a. oatcake
   b. oatmeal
   c. granola

UNIT 12

31. Circle the correct proposition.

a. Whisky, vodka, gin, rum, and brandy are:

1. spirits
2. soft drinks
3. mocktails

b. La petite quantité de whisky qui s'évapore du fût lors de sa maturation s'appelle :

1. the moor's share
2. the devil's share
3. the angel's share

c. The wooden barrel in which whisky matures is called:

1. a keg
2. a cask
3. a safe

d. The acronym used to describe the percentage of alcohol in spirits is:

1. ABV, for Alcohol By Volume
2. ABU, for Alcohol By Unit

32. Les mots en gras sont placés dans la mauvaise phrase, remettez-les à la bonne place.

a. This new job is not all milk and **cream** ➜ .... You will have tough moments too.

b. You're just jealous because his car is fancier than yours. It's a case of sour **raspberries** ➜ .... !

c. What are you so happy about? You look like the cat that got the **honey** ➜ .... !

d. I've just married, I've bought a beautiful house, and I'm on holiday. Life is a bowl of **grapes** ➜ .... !

e. Children like to pull a face and blow **cherries** ➜ .... with their tongues.

33. Circle the right word in these translations.

a. I went out with Paul and Mary last night, and I played *gooseberry – strawberry* all night! Je suis sorti avec Paul et Mary hier soir et j'ai tenu la chandelle toute la soirée !

b. My son has a *gooseberry – strawberry* mark on his left arm. Mon fils a une tache de vin (marque de naissance) sur son bras gauche.

34. Devinez le sens des expressions en gras en vous appuyant sur le contexte des phrases.

1. a headbutt, a blow given with the head 2. a scar-leaving type of wound on the face

a. Peter was injured in a car accident and has got a **Glasgow smile**. n° ....

b. John fought with Ian and gave him a **Glasgow kiss**. n° ....

UNIT 12

BACK TO WORK – LAUGH AND LEARN

35. Read the text below and then classify the a-g statements in the table.

The Scots have funny expressions, such as 'your bum is out of the window', which means 'you're talking nonsense'; and 'I'm getting the messages', which means 'I'm going shopping'. If they see someone who is wearing trousers that are too short, they will ask them 'has the cat died?'. But they also have an interesting word that does not exist in any other language: *to tartle*. The word is used when you bump into someone and you are about to say hello, but for a few seconds you cannot remember their name and you feel uncomfortable as a result: 'Hello mmmm… Tom! Sorry, I tartled there for a moment!'. To apologise they will sometimes say, 'Sorry for my tartle'.

The Scots are prone to eating fatty food, particularly fried food, and it comes as little surprise that they should have invented two of the most peculiar food things. One is the Munchy Box (a pizza box that contains nothing else but fast food: kebab meat, sausages, chicken nuggets, pizza, chicken tikka, onion rings, and chips). The box was first invented in Glasgow for young people to eat after a night of clubbing. And hold on to your hats for the second invention: the deep-fried Mars bar! Yes, a Mars bar rolled in batter and deep-fried like a chip! Just what the doctor ordered!

a. *Hold on to your hats* signifie *revenons à nos moutons*.
b. *Messages* can mean *groceries* in Scottish.
c. *Bum* is a Scottish slang word for *nose*.
d. *To tartle* means *to make a mix up about someone's name*.
e. *The Scots* have *a sweet tooth*.
f. *Peculiar* means *strange*.
g. *Just what the doctor ordered!* is used ironically here.

RIGHT	WRONG
n°	n°

36. Reliez chaque début de proverbe ou citation à sa suite, puis devinez comment se disent les mots donnés en dessous.

1. 'Scotland, the country where they fry the food
2. 'Put cream and sugar on a fly
3. 'Give a donkey oats
4. 'When you shoot an arrow of truth,
5. 'Bees that have honey in their mouths

a. and he runs after thistles.' (Dutch proverb)
b. have stings in their tails.' (Scottish proverb)
c. five times to make sure it's dead.' (Dylan Moran)
d. and it tastes very much like a black raspberry.' (American proverb)
e. dip its point in honey.' (Arab proverb)

A. chardon ....
B. mouche ....
C. dard ....
D. flèche ....
E. tremper (dans) ....

UNIT 12

37. Circle the correct meaning(s) of this English proverb. *'Whisky on beer, never fear. Beer on whisky, mighty risky.'*

a. Drinking beer after whisky is a little risky.

b. Drinking beer after whisky is really risky.

c. Drinking beer and then whisky is nothing to worry about.

38. Entourez le proverbe anglais qui signifie la même chose que le proverbe écossais *'No bees, no honey; no work, no money.'*

a. No brain, no gain.

b. No pain, no gain.

c. No rain in vain.

END-OF-CHAPTER TEST

39. Translate these sentences into English

1. Le cranachan aux framboises a toujours été privilégié par la plupart des gens, mais ce n'est pas mauvais non plus avec des mûres ou du cassis.

....

2. Les flocons d'avoine ont besoin d'être un peu sucrés. Assure-toi de les arroser d'un peu de miel juste avant que les invités arrivent (mais pas trop car sinon ils seront détrempés).

....

3. Je n'avais pas conscience du fait que les chardons s'épanouissaient pleinement dans un climat plutôt humide et froid.

....

4. On mangera du cranachan partout en Écosse d'ici la fin du mois, quand les framboises seront de saison. Nos papilles en frissonnent déjà !

....

5. Le miel, le whisky et les framboises sont des atouts majeurs pour l'économie écossaise.

....

SOLUTIONS

UNIT 1 - COLESLAW

1. Coleslaw is a side dish of raw vegetables whose main ingredient is cabbage. It's a popular summer salad in the United States and in Great Britain, where it is often eaten at barbecues along with various grilled meats. It can also be used to garnish sandwiches. The recipe dates back to the Dutch immigrant colonies on the east coast.
2. a. F **b.** F **c.** V **d.** F **e.** V **f.** F
3. b
4. c (travel est indénombrable)
5. b
6. a, c, d
7. b
8. b (signifie 'fade')
9. a, b
10. a, d, f, h, j, k
11. a
12. Let us not start our little food journey.
13. a
14. a. misadventure **b.** adventurousness
15. consumption
16. a. the **b.** Ø **c.** Ø **d.** the
17. b (recettes, commentaires sportifs : présent simple)
18. a. non **b.** oui
19. a. prepare – are preparing **b.** are not eating **c.** do you need **d.** does not approve **e.** are always having **f.** have consumed **g.** makes **h.** do you buy **i.** like – are eating **j.** comes
20. a. that, Ø **b.** what **c.** that, Ø **d.** which **e.** who **f.** that, which, Ø **g.** whose
21. a. apples **b.** vegetable **c.** food processor **d.** shredding blade **e.** side dish
22. a. for **b.** during **c.** while
23. a. does not **b.** no
24. 'as a salad', 'as a side dish' (l. 15 tous les deux)
25. a. like **b.** as
26. oui
27. a. either … or **b.** although **c.** despite **d.** in spite **e.** unlike **f.** whether … or
28. a. F (*sour* rime avec *hour*) **b.** V **c.** F [ˈrèizᵉᵘn] vs [ˈrizᵉᵘn] **d.** F ([ˈkabidʒ] vs [miˈrâʒ]) **e.** V (le e final se prononce [i]) **f.** V
29. example, carrot
30. étaient corrects : address, envelope, rhythm, syrup, luggage, aggressive, development, to pronounce; étaient incorrects : achieve, across, mirror, apricot, function, language, pronunciation, abbreviation
31. [ss] mustard, basic, close, consumed, also [ʒ] version, occasion [z] used, using [ch] sugar
32. a. le d **b.** le k **c.** le l **d.** le deuxième **e.** le l **f.** le i
33. a. kale **b.** cauliflower **c.** broccoli **d.** Brussels sprouts
34. a. This test was duck soup but he failed. His goose is cooked! **b.** Mind your own business or things are going to turn ugly. **c.** Ian is losing his temper because Sam told him he had cauliflower ears.
35. a. cabbage **b.** carrot **c.** cabbagehead **d.** salad **e.** onions
36. a3, b1, c4, d2
37. may
38. was (to be), thought (to think), gave (to give)
39. a. [d] **b.** [id] **c.** [t]
40. a. [ˈichiou] est plus courant et préférable, mais [ˈissiou] est une variante possible **b.** [inˈkriss] **c.** [ˈstamᵉᵘk]
41. may, digestive problems, you'd better, easy, tend to, advised, manliness, raise, disappeared, broadened
42. a. I would like (souhait) **b.** 1, 3 **c.** for **d.** ago **e.** since
43. nothing except, only, merely, just, simply, no more than, solely
44. a. on passe d'une absence d'obligation à une interdiction **b.** 1. a sexual innuendo about oral sex **c.** 2
45. I like men better than cauliflowers.
46. damned, bloody
47. 1. All (that) you need to make a good coleslaw dressing is the recipe which/that comes from my mother. Peel the carrots while I'm reading it to you. 2. Although broccoli is not children's favourite vegetable, they generally like cauliflower, which is surprising. 3. Potato salad and coleslaw are traditional side dishes in the United States, but they can also be eaten on their own. 4. I'm not eating raw vegetables such as crunchy cabbage at the moment because I often get (a) stomach ache. You'd better do likewise.

UNIT 2 – CLAM CHOWDER

1. not smooth but **chunky**, **fish soup** and not meat broth, Clam chowder is **typical of New England**, at the beginning chowder would be made **with any fish available, not clams only**. In Manhattan, people started making a version of chowder **using tomato, not corn**. Chowders are accompanied by small crackers called oyster crackers **but they are not filled with oysters**, and yes, you will be able to cook this dish if you cannot find fresh seafood.
2. a. an epitome **b.** a prawn **c.** a sweetheart **d.** cringe at **e.** warm **f.** available
3. a. scallop **b.** thoroughly **c.** escape **d.** chunky **e.** acquired taste **f.** sweat
4. c; 1. starter 2. main course 3. dessert
5. a. to have trouble **b.** it is highly probable **c.** to outlaw/to forbid **d.** to eliminate, to get rid of **e.** to fill the bill/to work **f.** misleading
6. a. unexpectedly **b.** contrary to **c.** yet **d.** though
7. 1 d, 2 f, 3 g, 4 b, 5 c, 6 e, 7 a
8. a. vraiment **b.** en réalité, en fait **c.** un jour, finalement (elle finira par…)
9. very
10. a. They feel like oysters. **b.** They smell like oysters. **c.** They sound like oysters. **d.** They taste like oysters.
11. a. of, for **b.** of **c.** in **d.** of, out **e.** from, for
12. are
13. a. n'importe lesquels **b.** aucune (absence de)
14. What are they called? (et non *how*)
15. 'you will find in chowder' (l. 7), 'you're going to have a hard time' (l. 23, 24)
16. a. I am about to start cooking the clams (3), **b.** There are some clams on the kitchen table. Mum is going to cook chowder. (4), **c.** Shall we make some chowder? (6), **d.** I'll have some clam chowder, please. (2), **e.** I am making chowder for our dinner party.(1), **f.** Will you help me with the cooking? (5)
17. a. you're not going to try **b.** will you invite **c.** you're not going to buy **d.** will you make
18. a. When you go to Boston, will you eat some chowder? **b.** By the time you arrive, the children will have finished their soup. **c.** This time tomorrow, we will have had chowder in Boston.
19. a. V **b.** F ([ᵉᵘbᵉᵘl] vs [ˈèībᵉᵘl] **c.** F ([prôn] [ˈbra-on]) **d.** V (mais 3 syllabes dans le Nord de l'Angleterre)
20. a. [i] seafood **b.** [â] sweetheart **c.** [è] sweat
21. stalk
22. a. [ˈaīᵉᵘn] **b.** [ˈstiou] **c.** [iˈpitᵉᵘmi] **d.** [ᵉᵘkouaīᵉᵘd] **e.** [ˈoīstᵉᵘd] **f.** [ˈsèd] **g.** [ˈkeumfᵉᵘt] **h.** [ˈbèïsst]
23. voir page 142
24. a. clam **b.** corn **c.** soup **d.** oyster
25. a. lobster **b.** skin **c.** limpet
26. a. 2 **b.** 2 **c.** 1 **d.** 3
27. Here are two astounding American laws:
- it's illegal to slurp your soup in New Jersey, so mind your manners!
- it's not allowed not to drink milk in Utah, so forget about your lactose intolerance if you suffer from it!
a. V **b.** F
28. aphrodisiacs, stamina, a day, careful, like, eggs, relieve, latter
29. *to pull a muscle* signifie *se froisser un muscle*, mais en langage familier, *to pull* signifie 'emballer quelqu'un' (sortir et coucher avec)
30. b
31. a. chief **b.** key **c.** major

135

SOLUTIONS

32. bold
33. c
34. a. shame **b.** pity
35. a. on **b.** for
36. c
37. b, d
38. a. chocking **b.** digging
39. reasoning, ability, convince, eating
40. 1. If you don't like mussels, I will make corn chowder for you - it's the epitome of vegetarian chowders. **2.** These crackers have a misleading/deceptive name and they are a funny shape, but they will do the trick! **3.** I'm about to brown some scallops. Leave the clams to simmer for ten minutes and bring the milk to a boil. **4.** Shellfish is an acquired taste but you will like it, eventually. **5.** Don't clam up, you are so young - the world is your oyster!

UNIT 3 – FISH AND CHIPS

1. a. Wrong, it's not a dish you eat at the restaurant but that you take away. **b.** right **c.** Wrong, a chippy is not a pub but a place where they cook fish and chips. **d.** Wrong, they stopped for health reasons. **e.** right **f.** Wong, it still is **g.** right
2. voir page 142
3. a. the nineteenth **b.** ten thousand **c.** two hundred and fifty **d.** the nineteen eighties
4. a. breakthrough **b.** drawback **c.** check-up **d.** runaway **e.** workout
5. a highly skilled cook, much needed sleep, hard-earned money, a kind-hearted friend, a narrow-minded neighbour, old-fashioned ideas, poorly cooked fish, a newly opened restaurant
6. a. enduring **b.** cod **c.** deeply-ingrained **d.** psyche **e.** lump-free **f.** over
7. a. 3 **b.** 1 **c.** 2 **d.** 2 **e.** 1
8. in, in, at, on, at, in, at, on, at, on, on
9. a. actions révolues : was wrapped up, gave rise **b.** action qui continue dans le présent : the dish has been the national pride
10. a. ran **b.** have just had **c.** did not eat **d.** have bought **e.** took over **f.** forgot **g.** have been … began
11. a. 1 **b.** 3 **c.** 2 **d.** 1
12. a. ago **b.** since **c.** for
13. Those are the crispiest chips (that) I have ever eaten.
14. a. I have peeled the potatoes. You can slice them now. **b.** I have salted the chips. They taste better now. **c.** I have bought fish. We can prepare fish and chips.
15. a. When I was a child, people would put vinegar on their chips. **b.** Fish and chips used to be wrapped up in newspaper. Habitude qui a cessé : phrase n° b ; Tendance au passé : phrase n° a. **c.** Fish and chips is not wrapped up in newspaper anymore. **d.** Fish and chips is no longer wrapped up in newspaper.
16. a. am used to making, haven't eaten, for, since, last, has been, since, ate **b.** didn't use **c.** used to, ago
17. a. had to peel **b.** were allowed
18. a. How long has fish and chips existed? **b.** Did you use to like fish as a child? **c.** When did you catch that fish? **d.** Have you heard about that chippy owner yet? **e.** How often did the oil in the fryer need changing? **f.** How far from the sea have you lived?
19. a. psyche **b.** wrap **c.** psyche **d.** fillet
20. b, d, e, f (*flour* se prononce comme *flower*, *lager* ['lag^{eu}], *lump* ['leump])
21. a.4 cod, b.1 trout, c.7 mackerel, d.6 salmon, e.8 skate, f.3 whiting, g.2 sea bass, h.5 tuna
22. a. fishbone **b.** gills **c.** smoked **d.** raw **e.** eel **f.** to shell
23. a. big **b.** queer **c.** small **d.** fishy
24. a. pea **b.** fish **c.** chip **d.** beer **e.** chip **f.** fish
25. a4, b6, c3, d8, e7, f2, g1, h5
26. a. homophone de 'our place' **b.** Oh my God (interjection) **c.** New Kid on the Block (célèbre boys band américain des années 80) **d.** Film *The Godfather* (Le Parrain) **e.** Chippendales **f.** *Finding Nemo* (Le monde de Nemo)
27. A. during, world, enemies **B.** mushy, side, most, ever, spare, rule, should, upwards, knife, side, law, mind, pyjamas, last, dead.
Mots cachés : voir page 142
28. twice
29. wise, strong
30. a. … the **most** delicious thing I have **ever** experimented. **b.** I still haven't experienced anything better **than** … **c.** The first taste of beer is the **only** thing that feels **so** good.
31. Teetotaler x2
32. c
33. help stopping
34. goes in, go out
35. 1. I used to hate mushy peas. **2.** Have you ever tried frying your chips twice? They taste better that way. **3.** I would order takeaway when I lived in Boston; on Friday nights mostly. **4.** 'Fish and chips' is a dish that has been important to the English psyche since it was invented in 1860. **5.** I found (some) inexpensive salmon and cod at the market a few hours ago, but I haven't been able to buy any tuna yet.

UNIT 4 – GLAMORGAN SAUSAGES

1. a. leek, vegetable **b.** prevents, wasting **c.** cheese **d.** look **e.** meat **f.** lies
2. a. Wales, **Welsh**, a **Welshman**, two **Welshmen b.** Denmark, Danish, a Dane, two **Danes c.** China, Chinese, a Chinese, two **Chinese d.** Spain, Spanish, **a Spaniard**, two Spaniards **e.** correct
3. a. leek **b.** sharp **c.** yolk **d.** oats **e.** stale
4. voir page 142
5. a. using up **b.** makes sense **c.** readily **d.** come by **e.** average **f.** piece of
6. a. 2 **b.** 1, 2 **c.** 2, 3 **d.** 1, 3 **e.** 1
7. academic**al**, energetic**al**, majestic**al**, biological, grammatic**al**
8. a. was cooking, called **b.** has had **c.** have eaten up **d.** have been frying **e.** have been living **f.** arrived
9. a. The sausages were already sizzling when I realized I had forgotten the cheese. Les saucisses étaient déjà en train de cuire quand je me suis rendu compte que j'avais oublié le fromage. **b.** It was the first time I had made Glamorgan sausages. C'était la première fois que je faisais des *Glamorgan sausages*. **c.** There was Caerphilly cheese, so I was able to cook real Glamorgan sausages. Il y avait du Caerphilly, j'ai donc pu cuisiner de véritables *Glamorgan sausages*. **d.** When I was younger I could chop leeks without tearing. Quand j'étais plus jeune, je pouvais émincer des poireaux sans avoir la larme à l'œil. **e.** What have you been doing lately? Qu'est-ce que tu deviens ? **f.** She has prepared Welsh food twice this month. Elle a cuisiné gallois deux fois ce mois-ci.
10. a. breadcrumb **b.** yolk, half **c.** sausage **d.** thyme
11. b. meet, meat (l. 5) **c.** beet, beat (recette, 2.) **d.** pour, poor (l. 6) **e.** maid, made (l. 7) **f.** mane, main (l. 3) **g.** time, thyme (recette, 2.) **h.** leak, leek (l. 3) **i.** flower, flour (recette, 4.)
12. a. montante **b.** descendante **c.** descendante **d.** descendante **e.** montante jusque breadcrumbs, puis descendante
13. a. rosemary **b.** oregano **c.** tarragon
14. a. cheese: runny, crumbly, sharp, mild, pungent, hard, spreadable, creamy, blue, ripe, moldy, melted, aged, wheel, block, lump, brick, log, wedge, slab **b. egg:** runny, scrambled, hard-boiled, sunny side up, poached, soft boiled, over easy, fried, shell, yolk **c. bread:** wholegrain, leavened, crumbly, sliced, crusty, stale. Toast, soldiers, bun, slice, loaf, crumb, roll. "Runny" signifie « coulant », il peut donc s'utiliser pour un œuf ou pour du fromage. "Crumbly" signifie « friable, qui s'émiette facilement », on peut donc l'utiliser pour du fromage ou du pain.

SOLUTIONS

15. a3, b5, c1, d2, e4
16. a. bread **b.** egg **c.** cheese **d.** sausage
17. a. cheese **b.** bun **c.** butter **d.** sausage
18. Sausages look **like** penises and **when** it comes to sausage-related **sexual** euphemisms, we are all **suddenly** back to **being** silly twelve-**year**-olds once again... English is **no** exception and 'to **hide** the sausage' for **instance** means 'to have sex' (nudge nudge, wink wink...). Now that you know **this** essential **information**, let's continue with funny cheese facts, shall we?
19. a. all of a sudden **b.** to have (sexual) intercourse **c.** to move on
20. a. F ['iou^{eu}miz^{eu}m] **b.** V **c.** V **d.** V
21. a5, b3, c6, d2, e4, f1
22. a. dairy **b.** fantasy **c.** slightly **d.** hole **e.** factory
23. In England there is such a thing as cheese rolling competitions - People roll a huge wheel of cheese down a hill and run after it in an attempt to get it first. The most famous cheese rolling takes place in Brockworth, where the cheese is rolled down Cooper Hill. In the smaller village of Randwick, three wheels of cheese are rolled round the church. When the competition is over, the villagers all snack on one wheel. The legend says that sharing it will bring protection to the village.
Mots croisés : Voir page 142
24. a4, b3, c6, d5, e1, f2
25. a. grief **b.** plain **c.** physician
26. a. on **b.** of **c.** for
27. a. Welsh **b.** Dutch **c.** Welsh
28. to wash up = faire la vaisselle
29. a. dark **b.** dart **c.** fart (signifie 'pet')
30. 1. I was making breadcrumbs with the stale bread when I remembered that I needed (some) nutmeg for the recipe. 2. No wonder (that) your parents did not like your recipe with strong cheese. They stopped eating dairy ten years ago. 3. It's the second time I have cooked a leek omelette this week. I could cook Welsh food when I was young. 4. He had given me this piece of advice; to add two yolks and a piece of crumbly cheese in. 5. This information about Welsh food makes sense to me.

UNIT 5 – BAKED BEANS

1. a. wrong (from Boston, U.S.A.) **b.** wrong ('altogether different' = totally different) **c.** right **d.** wrong (they are fond of them, they are still a top-selling food there) **e.** right **f.** wrong (it prevents getting stomach ache)
2. a. delightful **b.** Boston **c.** hearty **d.** fuel **e.** cuppa **f.** kettle **g.** splash
3. voir grille 142
4. a. sauce **b.** Boston
5. a. everyday, every day **b.** all together, altogether **c.** the former, the latter **d.** on the one hand, on the other hand
6. a. 2 **b.** 1 **c.** 2 **d.** 2 **e.** 3 **f.** 2
7. a. Besides **b.** Insofar as **c.** hence **d.** yet
8. a. upset **b.** painful **c.** sore
9. unfair, underestimated, misunderstanding, disapproval, overestimated
10. a. top-selling (l.7) **b.** low-budget (l.1)
11. on
12. a. chose **b.** bind **c.** few **d.** is good
13. a. can **b.** slice **c.** lump **d.** pinch **e.** plate **f.** mug **g.** carton **h.** chunk or side **i.** bunch **j.** stick
14. I was too busy discuss**ing** ... They make me **fart** ... But rather than **wait** ... Well I regret **doing** that ... everybody can afford **to** make baked beans. ... is far from **being** common in the U.K.
15. a5, b6, c4, d2, e3, f1
16. a. Ø make **b.** to use **c.** to buy **d.** cooking
17. Trying the full English breakfast is a good idea.
18. a. wrong (['lat^{eu}'] ['lèït^{eu}']) **b.** wrong (c'est l'inverse) **c.** right **d.** wrong (le ed se prononce [t] dans *baked* et [id] dans *naked*)
19. a. [**â**] hearty **b.** [**è**] instead **c.** [**i**] least
20. sugar (ne contient pas le son [j])
21. [tch]: approach, choose, chopped [k]: character, orchestra, architect, chaos, psychology, stomach, monarch, psyche, chemistry, mechanic [ch]: chalet, chauffeur, chic, machine, moustache
22. a. The full '**breakfast** with '**bacon** and eggs is '**filling**. **b.** Did you '**leave** your cup of '**tea** on the '**table**? **c.** Beans on '**toast** is not a '**staple** in '**Germany**. **d.** I for'**give** '**them**, but I don't for'**give** '**you**. (les pronoms sont généralement non accentués, exception ici car l'interlocuteur fait un contraste)
23. b
24. pulses
25. a2, b4, c3, d1
26. a. kettle **b.** bean **c.** tea **d.** bean **e.** tea
27. a. beanbag **b.** jellybean **c.** beanie
28. b. sin **c.** wind **d.** Easy **e.** motor **f.** Emerald **g.** Apple
29. a. bathroom humour **b.** cheese, biscuit **c.** fart around **d.** old fart **e.** brain fart **f.** waste **g.** toot **h.** biscuit
30. a. at, have any **b.** men know, their own farts **c.** to understand **d.** to
31. a. starve **b.** fears **c.** wind
32. a. tobacco **b.** 1
33. 1. I've made authentic Boston baked beans for a few years. I use a little molasses in my recipe and I add a nice splash of vinegar as well. I would not eat the English recipe for all the tea in China! 2. Students cannot afford to make dishes that are too expensive. Beans are convenient when you are on a (tight) budget and when you are not feeling like cooking. 3. On the one hand, I like the full English breakfast with its toast and its fried eggs; on the other hand I hate black tea. I prefer green tea, whose taste is altogether different. 4. The children prefer the sweet and thick sauce of Boston beans to the British recipe, particularly with their bangers and mash. Can you help me peel the potatoes? I'm busy frying the sausages. 5. My uncle Ted is an old fart. He renounced eating beans because he says that they give you an upset stomach.

UNIT 6 – SHEPHERD'S PIE

1. speak, warming, classic, embraced, ups, countryside, potatoes, cheese, top, cottage, instead, dieting, mashable, dark, companion
2. a. W (pumpkin is a type of squash) **b.** W (they do not think it is out of the ordinary) **c.** W (it was a way to use up leftovers) **d.** R **e.** W (it's added in step 2.)
3. voir page 142
4. a. decade **b.** pumpkin **c.** shepherd **d.** beverage **e.** stout **f.** sparkling water
5. a. to wash down **b.** your approval **c.** not one hundred percent **d.** ground beef **e.** agrees on **f.** in any case
6. c
7. a. Rufus's (ou Rufus', prononcé ['rou-f^{eu}ssiz] dans les 2 cas) **b.** parents' parents **c.** summer's night **d.** Jack and Donna's kids (s'ils les ont eus ensemble), Jack's and Donna's kids (s'ils ont chacun des enfants de leur côté et non en commun) **e.** children's
8. a. 3 **b.** 1 **c.** 2 **d.** 3 **e.** 1 **f.** 3
9. a6, b3, c5, d2, e1, f4
10. would have used ... had told
11. a. You had better not smoke so much. **b.** If I were you, I would not smoke so much. **c.** I would advise you not to smoke so much.
12. étaient mal orthographiés (quelques-uns sont des révisions...) : address, carrot, mirror, literature, across, beginning, apricot, language, syrup, function, to lose, dilemma
13. The British say 'mince' whereas Americans say 'ground beef.'
14. lamb, crumb, climb, plumber, thumb
15. 0: kind, lie, stir 1: cottage, mince, recipe (USA), celery, experiment (USA), beverage, complete, knowledge, business, secret, private, ideal, gene 2: recipe (GB), particularly, minute, equivalent, filling, biscuit, experiment (GB), original, women, media 3: aucun
16. a, c, f (*minute* ['minit], *cottage* rime avec *fridge*, *squash* ['skôch], *spinach* ['spinitch])
17. healthier (le ea se prononce [è], [i] dans

137

SOLUTIONS

tous les autres)
18. a. knight (chevalier) **b.** whine (geindre, se plaindre) **c.** pi (nombre 3.14)
19. a. 4 (3 dans le nord de l'Angleterre) **b.** 4 en général ['djén^{eu}rli] mais parfois 3 ['djénr^{eu}li] **c.** 3 **d.** généralement 3 ['i**ou**j^{eu}li], parfois 4 si parlé lent ['i**ou**jou^{eu}li]
20. a. 2 **b.** 2 **c.** 1
21. a. 'perfect **b.** he'llo **c.** 'carrot **d.** 'sparkling **e.** 'turnip **f.** car'toon **g.** Chi'nese **h.** 'decade **i.** 'comfort **j.** a'cross **k.** trai'nee **l.** 'winter **m.** a'broad **n.** 'shepherd **o.** Ju'ly **p.** 'mutton **q.** 'butter **r.** 'cottage **s.** e'nough **t.** un'real
22. a. veal **b.** mutton
23. a. girl **b.** rich **c.** above **d.** vet **e.** young → GRAVY
24. ++ overdone, well-done, medium, underdone, rare, raw - -
25. ++ whole, semi-skimmed, (skimmed) - -
26. chop
27. a. Cheddar **b.** Stilton **c.** Shropshire
28. a. 3 **b.** 1 **c.** 1 **d.** 2 **e.** 2
29. a. ewe **b.** ox
30. a. beef **b.** meat **c.** meat **d.** mince **e.** beef
31. a3, b1, c5, d2, e4
32. a et d, signifie *immédiatement, tout de suite, en un clin d'oeil*
33. c
34. a. tap **b.** still **c.** holy **d.** running **e.** sparkling **f.** spring **g.** drinking
35. a. water **b.** beer **c.** tea **d.** wine **e.** water
36. a. The Bunch of Carrots **b.** The Jolly Taxpayer **c.** The Cow and Snuffers **d.** The Drunken Duck and The Dirty Duck **e.** The Goat and Compasses **f.** The Goat and Tricycle **g.** The Snooty Fox **h.** The Idle Cook **i.** My Father's Moustache **j.** The Moody Cow **k.** The Bucket of Blood
37. c, e, a, d, b
38. a. fine, queer **b.** trouble **c.** improve **d.** guests, shepherds, hopeless
39. a. cook **b.** stuff
40. d
41. c
42. 1. Could you stir the veal stock and simmer the beef? **2.** If only Angus's (ou Angus) children liked turnips and pumpkin, I could have made mash for them, with a nice handful of grated cheese to make it all more appealing, and it would be in the bag! **3.** If you had told me that you wanted me to drive you to the station this afternoon, I would have had my dish with sparkling water and not stout. I wish I had known sooner. **4.** For decades, thousands of English households have lived on mashed potatoes and a little beef mince alone, as it were. **5.** If I were you, I would use up the mutton and the lamb leftovers to make some *shepherd's pie*. It's high time we stopped wasting so much food.

UNIT 7 – CHICKEN TIKKA MASALA

1. a. R **b.** W (it's a spicy sauce, the marinade is yoghurt-based) **c.** R **d.** R **e.** W (it may = it is possible, but not sure at all) **f.** W (it's a mild version)
2. voir page 143
3. favorite, flavors
4. a. to **b.** for **c.** to **d.** for **e.** to **f.** for **g.** to **h.** for
5. a. area **b.** era **c.** between **d.** among **e.** sensible, sensitive
6. 1. do: shopping, yoga 2. make: a plan, friends, a mistake, a promise, a decision 3. take: a ride, a picture, an exam, a nap, a seat, advantage, a break, care 4. have: a feeling, a laugh, a doubt, a break, a fight, sex, the flu 5. go: shopping, for a walk 6. keep: posted, a promise, calm
7. on
8. Henry, Olivia
9. a. Paula **b.** Erika **c.** Tess **d.** Suzie
10. a. 4 **b.** 5 **c.** 1 **d.** 3 **e.** 2
11. a. Ø **b.** yourself **c.** one another **d.** themselves **e.** Ø **f.** yourself **g.** himself **h.** Ø **i.** Ø, Ø, each other
12. a. would (si vous préférez opter pour...) **b.** had (tu ferais mieux de boire de la bière)
13. a. Had you better use much chilli? You had better not use much chilli. **b.** Would she rather add more garlic? She would rather not add more garlic.
14. le + : Liam le - : Ted
15. a. 2 **b.** 1 **c.** 4 **d.** 3
16. a. You ought to respect table manners. → 3 **b.** You'd better see a doctor as soon as possible. → 6 **c.** Maybe you should eat less for a while. → 1
17. a. If you do not use coconut cream, your tikka will be too dry. **b.** Unless you use coconut cream, your tikka will be too dry. (NB : on passe de 'is going to' à 'will' car la condition nécessite l'usage de 'will' pour exprimer le futur dans la proposition qui suit)
18. a. needn't **b.** might/should **c.** could, able to **d.** must **e.** would
19. a. You needn't use much coriander **b.** Need I bring some chilli?
20. a. back on **b.** keep off **c.** more and more; fewer and fewer **d.** more **e.** some **f.** the less, the milder
21. a. an **b.** a
22. a. weak **b.** plane **c.** chilly
23. bulk (le l se prononce)
24. [aɪ]: mild, rice, spicy, side, wine, [i]: minutes, grilled, minty, liberal
25. a. [i^{eu}] : unclear, European **b.** [è] : breasts, breads
26. on entend [ch] partout sauf dans *chicken* [tch], *chilli* [tch] et *ginger* [dj].
27. d, e (curry ['keuri], era ['ir^{eu}], beloved [bi'leuvid])
28. in'vent et 'damage étaient mal accentués
29. eggplant (aubergine, parmi des céréales)
30. a. buckwheat **b.** starchy
31. a6, b5, c3, d1, e2, f4
32. a. 3 **b.** 2 et 3 **c.** 1 **d.** 3 **e.** 2
33. a. wing **b.** drumstick **c.** leg
34. a. safe, front → saffron **b.** cloves **c.** fennel **d.** nut, Meg → nutmeg
35. a. lentil **b.** eggplant **c.** cauliflower **d.** spinach
36. a. rice **b.** salt **c.** curry **d.** salt
37. a. fowl **b.** turkey **c.** duck **d.** chicken **e.** goose
38. a. 1 **b.** 2
39. a3, b2, c5, d1, e4
40. a. Indian **b.** Chinese **c.** Greek **d.** Indians
41. a. Some people who are **sick** ... Thanksgiving ... the **tradition**al dish ... is a **stu**ffed chicken, inside a **stu**ffed duck, inside a turkey! ... by a **cook** in Louisiana in the 1980s. **b.** gent**lem**en ... sho**ck**ing; in**dee**d ... horny and re**sort** to the terrible ... were advised to avoid ...
as anti-masturbation **weap**ons, in an a**tt**empt to calm down m**en**'s **sex** drive!
42. a. fly **b.** rear **c.** illness, grief
43. a. lay **b.** a
44. a. weep **b.** properly, ripe **c.** stink, mistakes, single
45. Certains mots singuliers en 'ouse' ont un pluriel en 'ice' (comme *mouse, mice*). Ceci n'est pas le cas de *spouse* (spouses), mais l'auteur sous-entend ici que la polygamie épice la vie de couple.
46. a. true, way **b.** chicken, talk **c.** count, accurately
47. a et c
48. 1. It is unlikely that the children will not like your Indian meal. On the contrary, they love poultry breasts, particularly those of turkeys and chickens. Besides, they are crazy about your coconut milk smoothie. **2.** Your dish may be too spicy if you add pepper to it. You'd better put less pepper but a little more garlic in. **3.** You needn't crush the ginger; I have already done it. Relax and have a pale ale. **4.** What do you mean, 'it tastes like saffron'? It can't do. It **is** written *paprika* on the pot! **5.** My husband is very sensitive to strong spices. They give him a headache. The stronger the spices, the more intense his headache gets. Cinnamon does not hurt him, though, because it is rather mild.

SOLUTIONS

UNIT 8 – DUBLIN CODDLE

1. a. Coddle is a very simple dish associated with the city of Dublin. **b.** The dish has got many advantages and almost no drawbacks. **c.** Coddle is a type of comfort food appreciated during the colder months of the year **d.** It is customary to pair coddle with the famous Irish stout.
2. a. the Emerald Isle **b.** the Black Nectar
3. a. craic **b.** filling **c.** remove **d.** bottom **e.** store
4. a. wonder **b.** lid **c.** wallet **d.** share **e.** simmer
5. a. paying enough **b.** too much **c.** too busy **d.** can't-fail **e.** made **f.** trouble **g.** any unfortunate **h.** greater
6. a. 1. the 2. the 3. Ø 4. the 5. the 6. the 7. Ø 8. the 9. the 10. the 11. the 12. the 13. the **b.** 1. Ø 2. Ø à l'écrit mais on dira 'on November the 23rd' à l'oral 3. Ø 4. Ø 5. Ø 6. the 7. the 8. Ø 9. Ø 10. Ø 11. Ø 12. the 13. the 14. Ø
7. a. pros **b.** take **c.** hustle **d.** quiet **e.** sound **f.** loud **g.** sick **h.** wear **i.** span **j.** do's **k.** ends **l.** grey
8. A. a sweet smelling (a4) B. time saving (b6) C. a long lasting (c1) D. right handed (d3) E. a twelve recipe (e7) F. a second hand (f2) G. long haired (g5)
9. a.
10. a. Ø **b.** from **c.** for **d.** Ø **e.** on **f.** Ø **g.** for **h.** in **i.** on **j.** in
11. a. out **b.** in **c.** on **d.** to, to **e.** off
12. a. correct **b.** Coddle keeps Ø well for a few days. **c.** The potatoes **are** the same size. **d.** correct **e.** They should discuss Ø the recipes. **f.** Wait **for** me, please. **g.** correct **h.** correct **i.** He told Ø me he was a Vegan. **j.** Have you **told them** you were Irish?
13. a. on **b.** in **c.** at
14. a. isle **b.** autumn **c.** would et half **d.** chef
15. c. ['pâsli] ['greɪ]
16. étaient bien accentués : 'emerald, in'gredients, po'tatoes, 'sausages, 'nourishing, ca'thedral, 'difficult, dis'honest, va'nilla, 'celery, A'merican, 'consequences, over'whelmed. correction des autres : 'family, 'possible, ba'nana, 'yesterday, No'vember, e'leven, 'vegetables
17. Les noms composés sont accentués sur le premier mot (précision : en général)
18. a. cooked **b.** raw **c.** smoked **d.** chop **e.** lardoons
19. d
20. a. 5 **b.** 6 **c.** 4 **d.** 1 **e.** 7 **f.** 2 **g.** 8 **h.** 3
21. a. 4 **b.** 5 **c.** 1 **d.** 3 **e.** 2
22. a. in a pig's whisper **b.** couch potato **c.** salt of the earth **d.** hot potato **e.** bacon **f.** salt
23. 1. b 2. a
24. a. faux, se prononce *crack* **b.** faux, c'est juste un qualificatif **c.** faux, cela signifie qu'on s'amuse bien avec cette personne **d.** vrai **e.** vrai **f.** faux, quelques verres mais pas forcément un repas
25. d
26. voir page 143
27. a. wasted **b.** exhausted **c.** plastered **d.** angry **e.** behaviours
28. a, c, d (Crubeens = pieds de porc frits ; Barmbrack = pain aux raisins secs)
29. c
30. a. drink (Dublin, real, Italy, North, kitchen), punch (Patrick, uncle, November, cold, half) **b.** whiskey (week, hour, ill, slow, kiwi, easy, yummy) **c.** ladder (London, alive, dinner, dollar, empty, rain)
31. 1. I wonder if you will be able to resist this slow-cooking stew. It is very filling and it keeps well for several days. 2. I wish I had shared this meal with you. Unfortunately I have been overwhelmed this week. Don't wait for me for dinner. 3. I'm sick and tired of the chef burning all the saucepans' bottoms. Look at that, the onions are overcooked again. I don't trust him. What's more, the kitchen is not clean. It should always be spick and span. The restaurant's reputation is at stake! 4. He explained to me that you should not take the lid off right away but wait for at least an hour. It's the only drawback of/to this recipe.

UNIT 9 – APPLE & PLUM CHUTNEY

1. a. Chutney is a very generic term for two types of condiments: spicy or sour ones. *Faux Il peut avoir toutes les saveurs possibles et imaginables.* **b.** It is customary to serve a little chutney with meals in India. *Vrai* **c.** Chutney is commonly served alongside a classic pub dish called ploughman's lunch. *Vrai* **d.** Chutney is a fastidious condiment as it can only be used with few specific foods like meats. *Faux, il est très polyvalent et se marie avec tout.*
2. a. spicy **b.** sweet **c.** fruity **d.** sour **e.** minty **f.** tangy **g.** citrusy
3. voir page 143
4. a. endless, countless **b.** 3 **c.** cooking apples
5. a. versatile **b.** enhance **c.** soften **d.** dip **e.** ploughman **f.** cool **g.** smooth
6. a. as a result **b.** almost **c.** hardly **d.** for **e.** from **f.** efficient **g.** why **h.** better
7. as
8. a. and **b.** or **c.** and **d.** or **e.** and **f.** and **g.** and **h.** and
9. far
10. a. Ø (*a* est possible également ici, avec le sous-entendu 'type or recipe of chutney'), Ø
b. a, the **c.** an **d.** a, a, Ø **e.** Ø, a, Ø, the
11. a. a sense of humour **b.** correct **c.** has become an entrepreneur … what a wonderful surprise **d.** have a tendency
12. a. good, well **b.** well **c.** right, right **d.** good, good **e.** well, right
13. a. I usually drive to work on Mondays. **b.** My boss has worked himself sick **c.** The neighbour's dog ran away. **d.** I have scrubbed the chutney pot clean. **e.** You have talked me into making chutney. **f.** He threatened me into quitting.
14. a. up, into, down **b.** back, on, off **c.** off, up, on **d.** after, out, to
15. a. into **b.** across **c.** out **d.** to **e.** up **f.** out **g.** off
16. a. Give it up **b.** Take them off
17. a. 4 **b.** 1 **c.** 3 **d.** 5 **e.** 2
18. a. le gh **b.** le t **c.** le m
19. a. wrong (se pronounce comme *poor*) **b.** wrong (le ed dans *cored* se prononce [d] et [id] dans *pitted*) **c.** wrong (il est vrai que ces suffixes ne déplacent pas l'accent mais certains mots étaient par conséquent mal accentués : on aura 'readable, 'eating, 'tasted, 'freedom, 'lightly, 'happiness)
20. fruit, sugar, smooth, cooling, flew (autres sons ; sour ['saou^eu], flavours ['flèɪv^eu z], plum ['pleum], pour ['pô'], blood ['bleud])
21. a. seal (seal, même orthographe) **b.** pour (poor) **c.** cored (chord) **d.** wait (weight)
22. a. 2 **b.** 3
23. a. colour **b.** Ireland **c.** tea **d.** right **e.** ugly **f.** season → CITRUS
24. lemon
25. voir page 143
26. a. lemons **b.** a fig **c.** an apple **d.** bananas
27. a. a plum **b.** apples and oranges **c.** spice **d.** cider
28. a. apple **b.** cheese **c.** bread **d.** apple
29. … it is **also** a type of music from the **Southern** Caribbean, that has a fast **beat**. It was **born** in Trinidad & Tobago, created by Indo-Caribbeans – the **descendants** of 19th century West Indies **immigrants**. The music has its **roots** in Indian folk music, and has incorporated calypso and soca. Chutney **used** to be **sung almost** exclusively by **female** musicians and singers, and the songs' **lyrics** were **mainly** religious… More **recently** chutney music has been enriched **with** other … chutney is also used to refer **to** various human body fluids, but we will not go there, yuck.
30. a. unless **b.** amazing **c.** provided **d.** thirst
31. a. from **b.** whether **c.** believe, believe **d.** gold
32. 1. I'm looking forward to tasting your mango and citrus chutney. I'm sure its tanginess works wonders with poultry. Go and get some. 2. Keeping these jars is worth it

SOLUTIONS

because they are very versatile. I personally use them to store my chutney. 3. As he pointed out, this is a can't-fail recipe, provided that you are using cooking apples and not eating apples. 4. Could you pour the chutney into the jars and seal them? This batch is a bit too smooth for my taste, never mind. Next time, try and put some dried fruit in. 5. You have talked me into using chutney more in my cooking on a daily basis. It is true that its uses are endless. The delight of a good chutney on crusty bread for instance is often underestimated.

UNIT 10 – LAMINGTON CAKE

1. a. There is a disagreement between Aussies and Kiwis over the origin of Lamington cake. **b.** Lamington cake layers sponge cake, melted chocolate, and shredded coconut. **c.** The con of adding jam is that it may be too much of a good thing. **d.** Irish coffee will bring the tasting of Lamington cake to a higher level.
2. Australia: Land Down Under, Aussies. New Zealand: Land of the Long White Cloud (par déduction), Kiwis.
3. a. 1 **b.** 2 **c.** 2 **d.** 2, 3 **e.** 2
4. voir page 143
5. a. who have **b.** sugar, enjoy
6. a. bitterness **b.** sourness **c.** boredom **d.** stardom **e.** wisdom **f.** ownership **g.** manhood **h.** emptiness **i.** childhood **j.** sickness **k.** sadness **l.** forgiveness
7. a. Their refusal **b.** Her explanation **c.** (Our) acceptance **d.** Your arrival
8. a. intimacy **b.** certainty **c.** fluency **d.** secrecy **e.** clarity
9. a. disturbing **b.** decisive **c.** significant **d.** appealing **e.** accidental
10. don't they?
11. let's
12. a. likes **b.** has, their **c.** like **d.** every Australian likes
13. a. will you? **b.** haven't you? **c.** do you? **d.** does she? **e.** aren't I? **f.** is it? **g.** don't they? **h.** did they? **i.** Didn't it? (didn't they? possible)
14. did it? (did they? acceptable)
15. a. montante (vraie question)
b. descendante (pas vraiment une question)
16. a. 3 **b.** 1 **c.** 5 **d.** 2 **e.** 4
17. a. I don't suppose you know. **b.** Let us not eat too much. **c.** He asked me not to add any jam. **d.** Not everybody likes Lamington. **e.** The cake was not big enough.
18. a. correct **b.** The first ten squares **c.** what the ingredients are. **d.** twice as big **e.** the cake was actually too small **f.** Your advice was good … twice as many cakes.
19. a. some **b.** any **c.** some **d.** any
20. a. to **b.** over **c.** to **d.** in **e.** on **f.** from
21. a. right **b.** whole **c.** pair
22. a, d (bowl ['b^{eu}oul]], powder ['pa-od^{eu}], indulge [in'deuldj], huge ['Hi**ou**dj])
23. a. 3 **b.** 2 **c.** 2
24. cocoa
25. c. (tangy ['tangi], dessert [di'z**eu**t]], desert ['dèz**eu**])
26. pas d'erreur
27. [^{eu}t]: chocolate, delicate, desperate, passionate, climate [èït]: to desiccate, to grate, to congratulate
28. a. iced **b.** dissolved **c.** shaped
29. a. spread **b.** chip **c.** dark
30. a. hazelnut **b.** peanut **c.** chestnut **d.** walnut
31. a. shop, zero, sad **b.** pub, lie, feta, ten **c.** pod **d.** bean
32. loose (loose tea = du thé en vrac, tous les autres mots sont relatifs au café)
33. a. 5 **b.** 4 **c.** 2 **d.** 1 **e.** 3
34. a. cake **b.** nut **c.** nut **d.** cake **e.** cake **f.** nut
35. a. 3 **b.** 1 **c.** 2
36. a. Weird means 'strange'. Vrai **b.** In Austria there is a coffee made with broccoli. Faux (it's in Australia) **c.** In some countries, coffee beans are collected from animals' poo. Vrai **d.** Broccoli coffee consists of powdered broccoli added to black coffee. Faux (it's added to a latte) **e.** Mixing raw eggs and coffee is not a new thing invented by workout addicts. Vrai **f.** Broccoli coffee is going to use vegetables meant to be thrown to the bin. Vrai **g.** People who exercise are putting cheese in their coffee. Faux (they are putting eggs)
37. b
38. a. 3 **b.** 1 **c.** 5 **d.** 2 **e.** 4 **a.** clever **b.** rotten **c.** shell **d.** nettles **e.** give up **f.** a quitter
39. a. swear **b.** wedding **c.** whiskey **d.** care **e.** take **f.** hips
40. b
41. 1. The acidity of black coffee is counterbalanced by the sweetness of brown sugar and whipping cream. 2. My children have a sweet tooth and cannot resist this melted chocolate cake. Neither can we. 3. The first two times I made Lamington I made a mess of it. I had bought just any grated coconut, which was lacking in crunchiness. 4. The cake is all flat, that's weird. You have forgotten to add the baking powder to the batter, haven't you? 5. My sister claims that the cake's name comes from Queen Victoria. I don't think so.

UNIT 11 – PEACH COBBLER

1. Cobbler is not a finger-food dessert (it's **eaten on a plate**). Cobbler is with **a top layer of dough**, not of peaches (the peaches are under the crust), and the **peaches are not crunchy** but have a 'melt in the mouth' texture (fondante). It is not characterized by the overwhelming presence of cinnamon but its **faint presence** (it is the opposite, présence discrète). Cobbler is not better eaten straight out from the oven (directement sorti du four) **but after cooling**, until lukewarm (tiède).
2. a. 3 **b.** 1 **c.** 5 **d.** 2 **e.** 4
3. a. terrible **b.** terrific
4. a. 3 **b.** 1 **c.** 3 **d.** 1
5 a, b, c
6. a. a few, some, five, Ø, few (imaginable en réponse à 'do you need many peaches or not?) **b.** Ø, enough, any, much **c.** no, little, some, a little, enough **d.** enough, any, little (sous-entendu 'there is much')
7. a. Ø **b.** it, Ø **c.** Ø **d.** Ø, it. **e.** it, it **f.** Ø **g.** Ø
8. You can't resist = It is impossible to resist = It is irresistable
9. a. On ne peut pas nier (il est indéniable) que ton cobbler est meilleur que le mien. **b.** Il est impossible de dire (de prévoir) quand les pêches seront mûres.
10. Rightly so
11. a. most, all **b.** every **c.** each **d.** all, most **e.** each **f.** most, all
12. a. to **b.** of **c.** on **d.** out **e.** on, to **f.** to **g.** with, to
13. a. worldwide **b.** likewise **c.** southern **d.** south of
14. a. Betty said that she had left Dublin the year before. **b.** Henry said that he would pick up the peaches the day after. **c.** Jim said that he could help you/me/us/them.
15. a. He admitted that he had been wrong. **b.** He advised us not to use too much cinnamon on. **c.** She suggested that we go out for some cobbler. **d.** I wonder where the peaches are coming from. **e.** We asked what 'melt' meant.
16. a. Tell me what your favourite fruit is. **b.** I wonder whether/if they need more peaches (or not). **c.** Do you know where the butter is? **d.** I asked him how ripe the peaches were. **e.** 'When will they visit?' **f.** 'Has she/he bought peaches (or not)?' **g.** 'Don't eat ice cream!'
17. crumble (le b se prononce)
18. a. *dough* ne rime pas avec *enough* car son ough se prononce [o] alors que celui de *enough* se prononce [af] **b.** *gooey* se prononce ['gou-i], il ne rime donc pas avec *way* ['ouèï] (mais avec *honey, funny*, etc.) **c.** *cinnamon* ne se prononce pas ['tchinam^{eu}n] mais ['sin^{eu}m^{eu}n] **d.** correct **e.** correct

SOLUTIONS

19. a. coarse (l. 12) **b.** aren't (l. 19)
20. étaient mal accentués : possi'bility, compo'sition, com'panion
21. a. orchard **b.** rhubarb **c.** apricots **d.** pears **e.** sweet butter
22. a. popsicle **b.** waffle cone **c.** sundae **d.** granita **e.** frozen yoghurt **f.** scoop **g.** Italian ice or gelato **h.** sorbet or sherbet **i.** topping
23. a. 5 **b.** 4 **c.** 2 **d.** 1 **e.** 3 A: go pear-shaped B: to be a peach
24. a. granulated **b.** caster, confectioner's, icing, powdered **c.** pearl **d.** cane, Demerara, Muscovado **e.** molasses
25. lump, tongs
26. a. cookie **b.** honey **c.** candy **d.** sugar **e.** honey **f.** sugar
27. a. eggplant **b.** cilantro **c.** cookies **d.** sweets **e.** chips **f.** crisps **g.** zucchini **h.** granola **i.** arugula
28. Based on the **assumption** that vanilla is the **default** flavour that most people **choose** when buying ice cream, the word vanilla has **come** to mean basic, **ordinary**, standard. It can carry negative **connotations** and mean **plain**, unadventurous, and **boring**. The word is **particularly** used in sexual contexts. The **missionary** position for **example** will be labelled as vanilla, and sex that does not **involve** any 'naughty' things such **as** fetichism or S&M may be **considered** by some as 'vanilla sex'. As for the word 'peach', it is often used as a **metaphor** for women's **buttocks** or private parts, and by **extension** it can also refer to sexual **intercourse**. **a.** dull **b.** breasts **c.** kinky **d.** behaviour, within
29. a. fuck off, gorgeous, ripe **b.** long, occasionally **c.** ripen, length
30. a, d
31. a. mind **b.** heart
32. 1. I wonder where the nutmeg and the cinnamon are. She said that she had put them in the top cupboard. 2. There's no denying that it is ideal when you can get nice and tender seasonal fruit, it's a no-brainer. 3. She asked, rightly so, if I would be able to walk for a long time on cobblestones with these shoes. 4. This cobbler, which is topped with nice and gooey pears, will be terrific served lukewarm with ice cream. 5. You're a peach, you have brought me some good apricots back from the market. If I have time, I will make some stewed fruit or a cobbler with them.

UNIT 12 – CRANACHAN

1. 1. subtle 2. well-known 3. ground 4. climatic 5. encapsulates 6. main 7. all the qualities 8. less than 9. necessity 10. avoid using
2. a. aware of **b.** taste buds **c.** soggy **d.** asset **e.** honey **f.** costly
3. Kim and Adam
4. voir page 143
5. a. tart **b.** oats **c.** trifle
6. run of the mill ('ordinaire', 'médiocre' alors que les autres signifient 'délicieux' ou 'appétissant')
7. a. a Scot **b.** a Pole **c.** Sweden, a Swede **d.** The Netherlands, a Dutchman **e.** Turkish, a Turk
8. b
9. a. 3 **b.** 4 **c.** 2 **d.** 1
10. ninety percent ['naɪnti pəˈsènt], ninety-two point five percent ['naɪnti 'tou 'poɪnt 'faɪv pəˈsènt], nine out of ten/nine in ten.
11. Raspick at co dot uk/oh nine, oh eight, double five, nine three, four oh.
12. a. about, in **b.** on, on **c.** at, on **d.** on, in **e.** of, in, of **f.** to, on **g.** in, by
13. a. Some Japanese chefs cook living fish. OR Some Japanese chefs cook fish that is alive. **b.** A scared dog can bite. OR A dog that is afraid can bite. **c.** Don't disturb a sleeping dog. OR Don't disturb a dog that is asleep. **d.** A sick person can be contagious. OR An person who is ill can be contagious. **e.** An only child can get bored. OR A child who is alone can get bored.
14. a. sound, wide **b.** greatly **c.** quite **d.** much **e.** deeply **f.** well
15. a. Le Cranachan a été **le tout premier** plat écossais que j'ai essayé. **b.** Il a exécuté la recette sous mes yeux (sous-entendu : je l'ai vu, **de mes propres yeux**)
16. a. are eaten **b.** was invented **c.** will be delivered **d.** have been picked up **e.** is being made
17. a. Gaelic is still spoken is some parts of Scotland. On parle toujours le gaélique dans certaines parties de l'Écosse. **b.** Cranachan is said to date back to the 18th century. On dit que le Cranachan remonte au XVIIIe siècle. **c.** I was told that you were Scottish. On m'a dit que tu étais écossais. **d.** The raspberries are nowhere to be found. Les framboises sont introuvables.
18. a. A new variety of raspberries has been discovered. **b.** A full basket of raspberries has been given to us. **c.** We were given half a basket of raspberries.
19. a. Your secret will be found out. **b.** The problem had to be dealt with.
20. a. A postcard from Scotland will be sent to us. **b.** I was given a vintage whisky.

21. a. 3 **b.** 1 **c.** 4 **d.** 2
22. a. 3 **b.** 4 **c.** 5
23. a. raspberry **b.** berry **c.** gourmet **d.** guest **e.** honey **f.** buds, customary, under **g.** place
24. le p ne se prononce pas
25. a. 2 **b.** 1 **c.** 2
26. a. faux (il ne se prononce pas dans *gourmet*) **b.** faux (se prononce [aɪ] dans *thrive* et *climate*) **c.** vrai
27. 'piz**za**, in'gredi**ent**, 'fam**ous**, com'put**er**, 'cli**mate**, 'Scot**land**, 'choco**late**, 'cin**ema**, 'in**stant**, 'chil**dren**, 'hus**band**, A'meri**can**, a'fraid, a'gain, 'en**ergy**, po'tato, 'acci**dent**, ba'nana
28. a. straw **b.** blue **c.** cran **d.** goose **e.** black
29. a. blackcurrant **b.** pomegranate **c.** cherry
30. b
31. a. 1 **b.** 3 **c.** 2 **d.** 1
32. a. honey **b.** grapes **c.** cream **d.** cherries **e.** raspberries
33. a. gooseberry **b.** strawberry
34. a. 2 **b.** 1
35. right: b, f, g **wrong**: a (signifie 'accrochez-vous bien'), c (signifie 'derrière', 'fesses', comme en anglais), d (ne consiste pas en l'utilisation d'un nom pour un autre mais en son oubli, ainsi que d'un sentiment de gêne), e (ils n'aiment pas le sucré mais les aliments riches en graisse).
36. 1c, 2d, 3a, 4e, 5b A. thistle B. fly C. sting D. arrow E. dip (in)
37. b, c
38. b
39. 1. Raspberry cranachan has always been favoured by most people, but it is not bad either (when it's made) with blackberries or blackcurrant. 2. The oats need a little sweetening. Make sure you drizzle them with a little honey right before the guests arrive (but not too much otherwise they will get soggy). 3. I was not aware of the fact that thistles fully thrived in a rather damp and cold climate. 4. Cranachan will be eaten everywhere in Scotland by the end of the month, when raspberries are in season. Our taste buds are already tingling (in anticipation). 5. Honey, whisk(e)y and raspberries are major assets for the Scottish economy.

SOLUTIONS

UNIT 2 – GRILLE 23

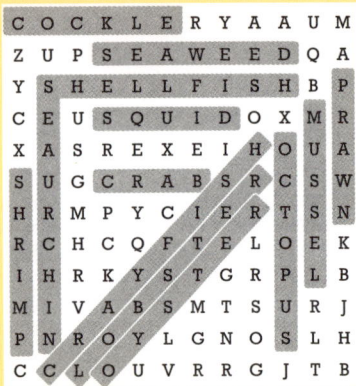

a. shellfish b. lobster c. cockle d. mussel
e. oyster f. squid g. sea urchin h. crab
i. seaweed j. prawn, shrimp k. crayfish l. octopus

UNIT 3 – GRILLE 2

UNIT 4 – GRILLE 23

UNIT 5 – GRILLE 3

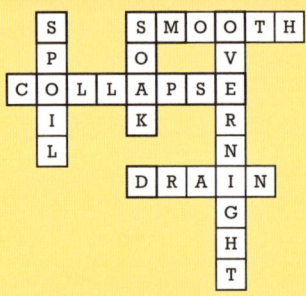

UNIT 3 – GRILLE 27

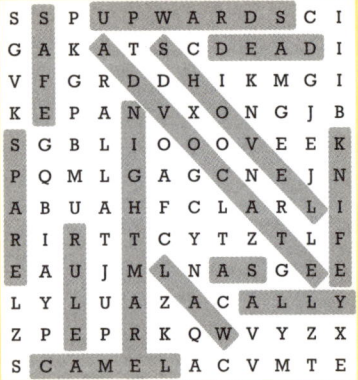

a. as b. spare c. nightmare d. upwards
e. shovel f. advocate g. safe h. law i. ally
j. rule k. knife l. camel m. dead

UNIT 4 – GRILLE 4

a. nickname b. seaweed c. allow
d. crumbly e. nutmeg

UNIT 6 – GRILLE 3

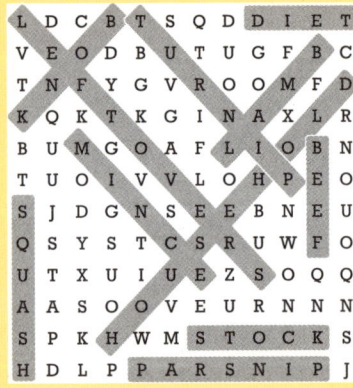

a. household b. beef c. squash d. turnip
e. diet f. lamb g. leftovers h. parsnip i. mince
j. stock k. knob

SOLUTIONS

UNIT 7 – GRILLE 2

UNIT 9 – GRILLE 25

a. raisin
b. fig
c. date
d. papaya
e. pineapple
f. mango
g. prune
h. quince

UNIT 8 – GRILLE 26

a. smurf b. Irishman c. previously d. oversimplify e. greet
f. mighty g. joking

UNIT 10 – GRILLE 4

a. joe
b. indulge
c. bone
d. claim
e. moistness
f. crunchiness
g. tangy
h. disturb

UNIT 9 – GRILLE 3

UNIT 12 – GRILLE 4

a. thrive
b. gather
c. oats
d. thicken
e. drizzle
f. frozen
g. Nessie
h. trifle

143

SOURCES

History and background:
Sarah Edington, *Complete Traditional Recipe Book*, National Trust, 2010
Annette Yates, *English Traditional Recipes: A Heritage of Food and Cooking*, Hermes House, 2014

Cooking tricks:
http://allrecipes.co.uk
https://www.theguardian.com

texte p. 13
Jennifer Evans, *BBC History Magazine*, April 2014
"When beans were the food of lust"

B. ex. 27 p. 34
Kate Fox, Watching the English, Hodder & Stoughton, 2014, pp. 442-443
https://shopkarls.com/blog/16-ridiculous-fishing-laws-will-make-jaw-drop/

texte ex. 21 p 42
https://foundinwisconsin.com/2019/02/wisconsin-state-laws-very-true-yet-strange/

texte p. 65
https://en.wikipedia.org/wiki/Pub_names

ex. 41 p. 77
https://www.dailymail.co.uk/health/article-3185011/What-Corn-Flakes-masturbation-common-Mr-Kellogg-believed-sexual-desires-caused-disease-invented-plain-cereal-stop-self-pleasuring.html

ex. 27 p. 89
https://www.theguardian.com/uk/2000/feb/25/jamiewilson

ex. 29 p. 100
https://en.wikipedia.org/wiki/Sundar_Popo
https://en.wikipedia.org/wiki/Chutney_music

ex. 36 p. 111
https://www.homegrounds.co/17-strange-yet-intriguing-coffee-experiences-that-you-must-try

ex. 35 p. 133
https://en.wikipedia.org/wiki/Munchy_box
https://www.telegraph.co.uk/foodanddrink/foodanddrinknews/8970054/Deep-fried-butter-balls-and-other-Scottish-delicacies.html

Les citations proviennent en grande majorité de
https://en.wikiquote.org/wiki/ (licence Wikicommons, Attribution-ShareAlike 3.0 Unported, CC BY-SA 3.0) ou sont utilisées avec mention de leur auteur dans le cadre du *fair use*.

CRÉDITS ICONOGRAPHIQUES :

Couverture
Plat 1 : Shutterstock : alazur : h-6 ; cheesekerbs : h-3 ; b-5dr : b-1, b-2, b-3 ; Everilda : h-1 ; Hein Nouwens : h-4 ; b-4 ; James Daniels : h-5 ; RedKoala : h-2 ; **plat 4** : Shutterstock : Vlad Klok : 1, 2 ; Fabulous Art : 3.
Intérieur
Shutterstock : 3D Vector : 38h, 105 ; Abscent : 52b ; alazur : 49, 91 ; Aleks Melnik : 23b ; Aleksangel : 2b-1 ; Alex_Murphy : 17b-1, 47b-2 ; Alexkava : 24b ; Aliaksei 7799 : 47h, 54, 125b-1, 127b ; Altana8 : 102b-2 ; Amin nur rochman : 116 ; Anna Chernova : 53b, 130 ; ArnaPhoto : 121, 123 ; Artem Stepanov : 3h, 27b ; Artur. B : 33, 8b ; astudio : 100 ; AVIcon : 115b, 118b ; Avny : 43b-1, 51, 90 ; bioraven : 8h, 10-1, 28-1, 45b, 47b-1, 52h ; Bobnevv : 38b ; brillianticon : 2h-3, 46h ; cheesekerbs : 17b-2, 22h-1, 22h-2, 23h, 24h, 29h, 57h, 67 ; Chistoprudnaya : 4b, 50h-2, 53h ; CosmoVector : 92b-2, 101 ; Everilda : 2h-2, 11, 15, 37h, 39, 57b-1, 70b-2, 122 ; Fabulous Art : 106 ; fad82 : 27h, 29b-1, 29b-2, 124b-2, 128h, 132 ; graphixmania : 25h, 25b, 41h, 56h, 57b-3, 58, 59, 109, 114h, 114b-1, 114b-2, 118h, 124b-1 ; grebeshkovmaxim : 131 ; green_01 : 125h ; grmarc : 61 ; gst : 17b-3 ; Hein Nouwens : 2b-2, 7h, 7b-2, 9, 13b, 14, 34, 36h-1, 36h-2, 36b, 37b-1, 46b-2, 48, 56b-2, 92b-1, 102b-1 ; HN Works : 119, 120, 125b-2 ; igorrita : 65, 89 ; Iurii Kiliian : 112 ; James Daniels : 19h, 19b ; josep perianes jorba : 107 ; Kapreski : 124h, 126 ; Katsiaryna Pleshakova : 2h-1, 3b, 6h-1, 21, 22b, 26h-1, 26b-1, 26b-2, 56b-1, 81b-2, 84, 93h-3 ; Kilroy79 : 103, 128b ; kristinasavkov : 37b-2 ; Ku_suriuri : 55, 66 ; Line - design : 92h, 96 ; LizavetaS : 46b-1 ; Marco's studio : 102h, 110b-2 ; Martial Red : 6b, 13h ; martin951 : 68b, 70b-1, 73-2, 74h ; Maxim Cherednichenko : 93h-2, 93b, 98h, 98b-1, 98b-2, 99h, 99b, 108, 115h ; MuchMania : 16b, 18h ; Nevada31 : 4h ; Nicolas Raymond : 44b ; nikiteev_konstantin : 50h-1, 110h, 110b-1, 110b-3, 113 ; notbad : 45h ; Oleg7799 : 20-2 ; openeyed : 104 ; Panda Vector : 18b ; Piter Kidanchuk : 43b-2 ; popcic : 97 ; PSNPJua : 127h ; Puckung : 20-1, 28-2 ; Ramil Ramiyev : 17h ; RedKoala : 16h, 41b, 42, 43h, 50b-1, 60, 69h, 70h, 73-1, 74b, 79 ; shutterstock dr : 94 ; Sunnydream : 75 ; T-Kot : 83 ; vectorisland : 50b-2 ; Victor Metelskiy : 57b-2 ; Viktorija Reuta : 6h-2, 10-2, 85 ; VKA : 77, 81b-3 ; Vlad Klok : 62h, 62b, 63, 64, 68h-1, 68h-2, 71, 78, 80h, 80b, 81, 81b-1, 86, 95b ; Vladimir Nosov : 44h ; YIK2007 : 95h

Directrice de collection : Hélène Bauchart
Conception graphique et mise en pages :
Laurent Quellet pour Lunedit
Réalisation : lunedit.com

© 2019 Assimil
N° d'édition : 3896
ISBN : 978-2-7005-0834-5
Dépôt légal : juillet 2019
www.assimil.com
Imprimé en Slovénie par DZS